FAIR STREETS ARE BETTER THAN SILVER
GREEN PARKS ARE BETTER THAN GOLD

☞ ☞ ☞

BAD PUBLIC TASTE IS MOB LAW
GOOD PUBLIC TASTE IS DEMOCRACY

☞ ☞ ☞

A CRUDE ADMINISTRATION IS DAMNED ALREADY

☞ ☞ ☞

LET THE BEST MOODS OF THE PEOPLE RULE

☞ ☞ ☞

A BAD DESIGNER IS TO THAT EXTENT A BAD CITIZEN

ADVENTURES
RHYMES & DESIGNS

ADVENTURES
RHYMES & DESIGNS

Including
the prose volume *Adventures
While Preaching the Gospel of Beauty*
together with *Rhymes to be Traded for Bread,
The Village Improvement Parade* and
selections from *The Village
Magazine*

BY

VACHEL LINDSAY

WITH AN ESSAY BY

ROBERT F. SAYRE

The Eakins Press *New York, Publishers*

TABLE OF CONTENTS

Vachel Lindsay   7
An Essay by Robert F. Sayre.

Adventures While Preaching the Gospel of Beauty   43
His prose account of his walking tour to the far West from his home in Springfield, Illinois.

The Village Improvement Parade   224
The series of picture-cartoons he gave away enroute.

Rhymes to be Traded for Bread   231
The pamphlet of his poems he distributed free.

The Village Magazine   247
Selections from the single issue periodical he published in 1910, and revised in 1920 and 1925, with other broadsides and leaflets.

Bibliography   283

VACHEL LINDSAY

An Essay by Robert F. Sayre

IN her memoirs Harriet Monroe describes her discovery of Vachel Lindsay. During the summer of 1912, when she was
combing magazines for potential contributors to her soon-to-
be published *Poetry: A Magazine of Verse*, she happened upon an
article in the *American Magazine* "by one Nicholas Vachel Lindsay
which referred to a pamphlet of rhymes he had exchanged for bread
and lodging at farmers' doors." Curious, she inquired in care of the
American, and in two weeks had an answer. The vagabond author,
now walking in the West, certainly did have verses to contribute
and was equally interested in her venture, which he called "an
Illinois enterprise." "I am emphatically a citizen of Springfield,
Illinois, and Sangamon County, and shall return in a year to stay
forevermore. If I may be confidential, I have been horribly home-
sick for a month—and fear that (spiritually speaking) I shall hob-
ble through the rest of my expedition." He would, he concluded,
send her something within the month.[1] The poem he sent was
"General William Booth Enters Into Heaven," and it was printed
in the January, 1913, issue, the magazine's fourth number.

The rest of the story is known—or used to be—to all readers of
Poetry, all disciples of "the new poetry," and to practically all students assigned anthologies of twentieth-century American poetry.
Vachel Lindsay (he dropped the Nicholas in 1915, at the recom-
mendation of his editors at Macmillan) was for a long time Harriet
Monroe's most famous "discovery"—"perhaps the most gifted and
original poet we ever printed," she said in her memoirs. The opening lines, "Booth led boldly with his big bass drum. . ." (with mar-
ginal notes explaining that they were to be "sung to the tune *The*

Blood of the Lamb [the Salvation Army hymn]. . . Bass drum beaten loudly"), sounded to hosts of readers like exactly the radical popular note they had been long awaiting. In November, 1913, "Booth" and William Butler Yeats' "The Grey Rock" won *Poetry*'s two prizes for its first year's contributors. There was to have been only one prize, but when Yeats was voted it, Miss Monroe obtained another for Lindsay. In March, 1914, at a *Poetry* banquet Yeats praised "Booth" warmly. "This poem is stripped bare of ornament: it has an earnest simplicity, a strange beauty, and you know Bacon said, 'There is no excellent beauty without strangeness.' " Later that evening Lindsay recited "The Congo."[2]

Lindsay's fame grew rapidly. In a short while he was reciting to English classes all over New England and the East—and to paying audiences in Carnegie Hall. "You must hear Mr. Lindsay recite his own 'Congo,' " Randolph Bourne wrote, "his body tense and swaying, his hands keeping time like an orchestral leader to his own rhythms, his tone changing color in response to the noise and savage imagery of the lines, the riotous picture of the negro mind set against the weird background of the primitive Congo, the 'futurist' phrases crashing through the scene like a glorious college yell,—you must hear this yourself, and learn what an arresting, exciting person this new indigenous Illinois poet is."[3] Herbert Croly, recognizing the connections between Lindsay's poetry and popular music, vaudeville, and the movies, asked him to write movie reviews for *The New Republic*. As a socialist, he sat at editorial meetings of Max Eastman's *The Masses*. As a pacifist, he was asked to sail on Henry Ford's Peace Ship. In February, 1915, at the opening of the Panama-Pacific Exposition, he recited his poem "The Wedding of the Rose and the Lotus" to members of President Wilson's Cabinet, and Secretary of the Interior Franklin Lane, his host, had copies of the poem distributed to members of Congress.

For once, it appeared, the new bard—"America's coming poet," as Secretary Lane grandly called him—was not going to be neglected and scorned. But, having first attracted attention as a vagabond, Lindsay was now to remain one, though at a different status,

8

for nearly the entire rest of his life. In January, 1919, he began the first of the long annual reading tours which were eventually to prove so bitter and exhausting. His audiences, contrary to the legend, were not usually women's clubs and businessmen but primarily college students and English teachers. He even recruited his own booking agent, A. Joseph Armstrong of the English Department at Baylor University, who between 1919 and 1924 proved very effective at arranging for such audiences, particularly in the South and Southwest. As he wrote Prof. Armstrong in 1922, "I will be a proud man indeed if I have blazed the way and made it possible for Frost, Sandburg, MacKaye and others to follow and go further than I have ever gone among the colleges and the Universities."[4]

I

YET it is fair to say, I think, that we now treat Lindsay as somehow very remote from us. His Bible-belt rhetoric, his association with old lost causes like foreign missions and the Anti-Saloon League, or his seeming Sunday-school innocence are aspects of an abandoned provincial America most people at colleges and universities are glad to be rid of. We are embarrassed by the tone of Harriet Monroe's effusive praise of Lindsay, her artful pressagentry, and her favoritism in obtaining prizes for him. Such praise from an editor who published the greatest poets of the century! We are also embarrassed, perhaps, by re-reading "The Congo" and "General Booth Enters Into Heaven." The enthusiasm of old anthologists that *this* is the real American poetry ("her characteristic rhythms") seems hollow. Other modern poets have not cared to be "washed in the blood of the Lamb," not Lindsay's lamb at any rate. Nor does "The Congo," with its subtitle "A Study of the Negro Race," seem the great liberal poem it was once considered.

Many readers would overlook Lindsay's obvious weaknesses, however, were his work more centrally "modern." His language and meters are novel and his subjects were unusual, but the work displays no interest in the imagination as a new means of inquiry. To him it was just a source of invention, not something which builds further perception or carries us to "new thresholds, new anatomies." There is no evidence that Lindsay ever read the French symbolists, or even read knowledgeably the work of his American contemporaries who were influenced by them. His direction was very different. Ezra Pound recognized the differences as early as 1915, when he wrote to Harriet Monroe, "I wish Lindsay all possible luck but we're not really pulling the same way, though we both pull against entrenched senility." A few months later, objecting to including Lindsay in the *Catholic Anthology*, he told her: "[Lindsay's] all right, but we are not in the same movement or anything like it. I approve of his appearance in *Poetry* (so long as I am not supposed to want what he wants), but not in anything which I stand sponsor for as a healthy tendency. I don't say he copies Marinetti; but he is with him, and his work is futurist." And later, "Lindsay's top ambition is obviously Kipling, which is all very well and good so far as it goes. Effervescence, futurism, it is very 'horrid' of me not to be enthusiastic about it. . . ." By October, 1915, opposed to another *Poetry* prize for Lindsay, he simply threw up his hands: "Lindsay . . . Oh gawd! ! !"[5]

Pound's complaints need little elaboration. Where Pound and the writers he championed were modernists, Lindsay was populist. He did not believe in an intellectual poetry but a popular poetry. Starting from about where Pound did — that is, from the Western political populism of the turn of the century, mixed with British aestheticism and an extremely ambitious definition of the poet's role — Lindsay turned to the then bright prospect of a broad, popular movement in twentieth-century art while Pound grouped his forces and eliminated quantity in favor of critical intelligence and quality. From our standpoint, over sixty years later, Pound's decision is the one which has prevailed. Modernism, at least in the Western nations, is triumphant, while populism, in both art and politics, is viewed with considerable suspicion. Recently, however, in numerous younger poets, among the new folk singers, and in many parts of the New Left, populism has shown important signs of life, a surge of liberality and hope missing from the established modernism. The direct indebtedness of this new populism to Lindsay himself is indeed small, and yet if we really want to re-open the case—to see what the old alternatives were, to find what strength populist art had, and to see where it went wrong—then clearly Lindsay must be re-examined. But to do so we have to try to see him in a large context, and in the process judge the context as well. For all his datedness or quaintness, Lindsay is still a great period poet, the sympathetic spokesman of that distant age of Bryan, Altgeld, and the rebellious miners and farmers; even though he himself was a middle-class boy from Springfield, with a first name that seemed like a girl's and a last that sounded like homespun linen and wool, a confusing and often confused mixture of things he was.

II

THE essence of Lindsay's populism was his walking tours. As the literary patriots immediately said, these trips were the experiences which gave him personal contact with the land and its people, and even less jingoistic admirers were excited by what he had done. Lindsay was fundamental: *Rhymes To Be Traded for Bread*—and he had walked the countryside reading poetry to farmers. But just as important, the walks changed Lindsay himself. The walks and the populist spirit were his own liberation from the genteel environment in which he had been raised. The actual transformation was clearly less than was later advertised, but the walks had still changed him from a prudish and ingrown provincial Pre-Raphaelite into a more tolerant and confident man. From there he went on to apply his poet's version of the vigorous life to poetry itself, thus also helping clear away misconceptions about the gentility of poetry. *Rhymes To Be Traded for Bread* was only a thin pamphlet with early Lindsay poems, most of which are now scarcely known. But in the process of trading them, he learned a little about which were the best and also moved towards the more emphatic styles which were to be his speciality.

Lest anyone think Lindsay was reticent about his walks, it should be quickly said that he publicized them all he could. The first was made in the spring of 1906 from Florida to Kentucky; the second in April and May of 1908 from New York to Ohio; and the third in the summer of 1912 from Illinois to New Mexico. In June, 1907, and January and February, 1909, five articles on the Southern walk appeared in the *Outlook*, a well-known weekly of religion and reform. The article in the *American* which Harriet Monroe saw was probably "Rules of the Road," which appeared in May, 1912. In fact, this progressivist monthly, founded by Lincoln Steffens and other muckrakers, also published Lindsay poems in three different issues of that year, and thus may deserve more credit for "discovering" him than *Poetry*. But in the *American* it was apparently the walks which placed the poems, for in August it published a sketch about Lindsay and his crusade which it had ordered from a more conventional contributor named Octavia Roberts, who lived in Springfield—and happened, by coincidence, to be Lindsay's girl friend.[6] As further publicizing of his walks, Lindsay had hoped that the *American* would print a series of "letters" from his 1912 Western trip. The opening of the diary kept on the trip indicates that one plan was for him to write as "Odysseus" to Miss Roberts as "Penelope."[7] When the *American* refused, however, he had to wait until *Poetry's* printing of "Booth" reversed the process so that his poems now increased interest in the walks. The letters home from 1912 appeared in the fall and winter of 1913-14 in the *Forum*, the literary monthly edited by Mitchell Kennerley, publisher of *General William Booth Enters Into Heaven and Other Poems*. It was these letters which were republished in book form later in 1914 as *Adventures While Preaching the Gospel of Beauty*, at the same time as the second collection of poetry, *The Congo and Other Poems*. In 1916 the materials on the earlier two walks through the South and Northeast were combined to make a second walk-book entitled *A Handy Guide for Beggars*.

12

In his walk-books Lindsay was appealing, in part, to a phase in American taste. In a general way, of course, the American impulses to "strike out for the open road" and to read books about roughing it, on the road, are apparently permanent. But around the turn of the century the number of writers going tramping and writing about it was unusually great. Carl Sandburg's time riding freight trains is well known. In the 1890's, however, even Robert Frost spent a few months riding freights through the South. Jack London described his time as a tramp in *The Road*, 1907. Other wealthier Americans wrote about life in Europe as tramps. The English poet W. H. Davies covered both England and the United States in his *Autobiography of a Super-Tramp* (1908), which was strongly praised by George Bernard Shaw and others. With the large number of itinerant laborers in the United States and the frequent industrial depressions, tramps were a pressing social problem, and some authors joined them from necessity, others from wanderlust and curiosity. Thus, in one sense Lindsay's walks were representative of a concern and tendency of his generation, like the movements of Dana, Melville, and Parkman towards the oceans and prairies or like the gravitation of a later group of writers into the World War I ambulance corps. And yet Lindsay's vagabondage was distinct from the others by being evangelical. W. H. Davies simply hated work and wanted to see the world. His final dream was a rustic cottage, good books, and a cheery fire. Lindsay, for better or worse, saw his walks as the commencement of a new gospel and the basis of his personal American epic. Like his populism, the walks were a crusade.

Behind that crusade lies a chapter in American cultural history which it is still very difficult to assess. It is not simply a consequence of Lindsay's late fame that his life has already been the subject of three long biographies.[8] Lindsay's life has that semi-mythic quality found in the lives of Sinclair Lewis, Sherwood Anderson, Dreiser, Fitzgerald, and Hemingway—other Middle Westerners of his generation and after, but novelists rather than poets. And certainly his small-town background, his exposure to the public schools and

evangelical churches, and his rebellion against small-town ugliness
and conformity had much in common with the general experience
of these other men. But where the novelists were "realists," which
for them became almost synonymous with expressing their disillu-
sionment with small-town culture, Lindsay was in essence a visionary, constantly divided within himself between what the Midwestern town was and what it *truly* was or somehow *ought* to be. Lindsay
was born in Springfield, Illinois, in 1879, the same year that Walt
Whitman, late in life, passed through Springfield on that excursion
to the Middle West which he told about in *Specimen Days*. The
coincidence is worth mentioning because, as everyone knows,
Whitman cherished that nearly universal nineteenth-century hope
in the Middle West as the essence of America, the heartland where
east and west, past and future, would eventually harmonize and
real democracy would grow. An example of this faith is Whitman's
little poem "The Prairie States."

> A newer garden of creation, no primal solitude,
> Dense, joyous, modern, populous millions, cities and farms,
> With iron interlaced, composite, tied, many in one,
> By all the world contributed—freedom's and law's and thrift's society,
> The crown and teeming paradise, so far, of time's accumulations,
> To justify the past.

Lindsay's fate was to be left with the burden of trying to work out
in greater detail what that vision meant.

This visionary optimism—rather than a sense of provincialism
or cultural inferiority—informed the Middle West of Lindsay's
youth. The answer to the charge of provincialism was that Springfield had produced Lincoln, and the town was full of Lincoln associations. Lindsay's parents had lately moved to a house at 603
South Fifth St. which had formerly been owned by a sister of Mary
Todd Lincoln; and, according to legend, the downstairs bedroom
where Lindsay was born had once been slept in by Lincoln (at any
rate, A. Lincoln)! A few blocks away, in a plain carpenter-architec-
ture similar to the Lindsay house, was Lincoln's own house. It was
a museum, but not yet "restored" in the fussy tastes of heritage

14

societies. Instead, the walls were literally covered with yellowing newspaper cartoons from the Civil War. One of Lindsay's cousins lived next to it, and the custodian allowed the two children to wander at large, listening to garrulous G.A.R. veterans reminisce and dispute. There, as around the Court House and Illinois State House, men still talked politics with that peculiar intensity observed by nineteenth-century European visitors, for politics *was* culture, in a way we no longer understand. The Illinois Governor's Mansion was next door to the Lindsay house. Lindsay's mother, an Indiana Republican, usually approved of the occupant, while his father, a Kentucky Democrat, usually disapproved, until the governorship of John P. Altgeld when the whole family approved. As a schoolboy, Nicholas Vachel kept a complete scrapbook on Altgeld, recording Altgeld's quarrel with President Cleveland, support of Bryan, and pardon of the Haymarket rioters with the interest children today devote to astronauts and movie stars, not state governors.

The political and social climate of the Middle West from about 1880 to 1910 was much more radical than many people now realize. Kenneth Rexroth has said recently of his boyhood in a small Indiana town, "People today have no idea how living a thing the Abolitionist spirit was as late as 1914. We can no longer gauge the destruction of native American radicalism and liberalism in the First World War." A family like the Rexroths (or like Lindsay's mother's, the Frazees) "were still animated by the spirit of a won revolution." To them the Civil War had been the working man's and farmer's hard victory over the twin evils of slavery and aristocracy, and their descendants felt a tremendous sense of confident egalitarianism. "It was from several generations who had won all their revolutions and expected to go on winning them that I came," Rexroth concludes.[9] Lindsay's family had some of the same spirit. His mother's energetic organization of missionary groups, reading circles, and temperance societies was not in the fashion of a clubwoman but a reformer. One of her family's stories was that her great-grandfather had taught Daniel Boone's children to read. Lindsay's father, though the son of a Kentucky plantation owner, had financed his own medical training, and then, accompanied by his sister and future wife, gone to Europe for additional study in Vienna and Paris. In their white frame house in Springfield, filled with books and the engraved reproductions of the European masters, they seemed ideal representatives of middle-class democracy.

There were, of course, corresponding qualities of complacency and benign optimism in such families—or, at any rate, so we now suspect. Lindsay's parents were members of the Disciples of Christ, a Protestant denomination with the confident fundamentalist view that disputes between other Christian churches were mainly the result of a failure to read scripture plainly and literally—the way the Disciples did. And yet one of Mrs. Lindsay's greatest achievements (in that day no small thing) was in uniting the work of all the separate mission societies in Springfield. She also staged masques and theatricals in Springfield churches. And in order to cope with his mother's strong convictions, Lindsay developed a stubbornness of his own, mixed with a sense of mockery and a way of going back to fundamental principles antecedent to hers and his father's. In a letter to his agent Professor Armstrong written shortly after his mother's death, Lindsay revealed some of these connections. "She was never," he said, "the mushy mellow and rabbit-like mother that appears in all movies. She was a holy terror to all those who were not prepared to dispute every inch of the way with her. To live with her was like being valet to the Pope in the Vatican and being a Protestant at the same time, making tactful efforts to conceal it." The point, obviously, is that Lindsay *was* prepared to dispute with her, both by being stubborn himself and by satirizing her excesses until (unlike the valet) he got what he wanted. Understanding this is very important. Lindsay combines stubbornness and humor. This is a quality of *Adventures While Preaching the Gospel of Beauty*, and it can also be sensed in the leaflets, pamphlets, and *War Bulletins* he published himself, directed at the philistines of Springfield during his four-year encampment there between 1908 and 1912. A slogan of the fantastic "Village Improvement Parade" is "To Begin We Must Have a Sense of Humor and Learn to

Smile." In other words, Lindsay's visionary parade possessed both determination and good humor. Lindsay quarreled with his town and with those stronger than himself like a laughing, very vigorous child. "All this is unreal, ugly, and silly," he seems to say, "and I may be just as silly to buck it, but you wait; I'm going to win; you see if I don't." It is the voice of a clever adolescent to his mother, whom despite their disagreements he still loves. And though it may seem pathetic and *is* childish, it does not have the other vices of the radical, such as arrogance or distrust. He will instead try *to charm* the evil away; for he believes, like a child, that people are good and that evil is too strong for anything *but* charms.

We can see these kinds of behavior in the first major crisis in Lindsay's life, the conflict with his parents over whether he was to become a doctor, and so follow into his father's practice, or go to Chicago to study at the Art Institute, as he wanted. The crisis came during his third year at Hiram College, a small co-educational college run by the Disciples. The quotations in the biography of Lindsay by Eleanor Ruggles from his letters home display his sense of art as a religious vocation ("My life is empty when I try to enjoy what the uncreative enjoy. . . . I must be in a creative mood, and I am *always* in some sort of creative mood . . .") and his sense of mockery ("I thought you would agree with me more. Don't be so panic stricken"). And so long as art meant so much to him—and could be defended in the religious terms which they had to recognize—his parents gave him their qualified blessing. Lindsay finished his third year at Hiram, where he genuinely enjoyed himself, drawing, writing, and happily participating in pranks and pep-rallies, and then six months later, on January 2, 1901, arrived in Chicago.

Up until his years in Chicago and New York, Lindsay's life was fairly typical, therefore, of the experience of many other aspiring small-town artists. There had been the affection for the town's more colorful figures over the respectable Methodists and Episcopalians, and there had also been Susan Wilcox, the young Wellesley-educated English teacher who had encouraged him and helped develop his rebellious attachment to Poe, Whitman, Blake, and

Browning as against the New England Immortals like Longfellow, Lowell, and Whittier. But in Chicago and three years later in New York he did not share other young men's ecstatic sense of liberation at the spectacle and promise of the great city. Lindsay remained solitary and loyally provincial. His notebooks record these years very completely, and they indicate how comparatively little companionship he had and how much time he spent by himself walking, strolling through galleries and churches, and closed in his room reading, writing, and dreaming. Where the more typical art student tried to become worldly and urbane, Lindsay became visionary and idealistic — traits which were of obvious importance to the walks and the populism. When he did sit with other artists in a bar, Lindsay drank sarsaparilla. Better yet was simply going out for ice cream. He knew little of the romantic bohemianism of the art student's life and much more of the drudgery of city workmen.

In his studies he was hampered by the necessity of taking dull jobs to support himself (or else feel guilty about depending on his parents) and by conflicts between art, poetry, and his messianic impulses. From September to December, 1902, in Chicago, he worked for $6.00 a week in the stockroom of Marshall Field's toy department. With the Christmas season his hours were extended from 8:30 a.m. until midnight, and on December 5 he gave up, having seen what that side of commerce was like. While in New York he worked for a time at a gas tubing plant owned by a friend's father. For a longer period in New York he taught classes in art history at the YMCA, having as students policemen and street car conductors. During his long hours in rented rooms he wrote down in his various little notebooks his many anxieties and ambitions. His original hopes, before going to Chicago, had been very egotistical and boyish, only chastened by the boyish self-mockery.

First year Chicago. Second year New York. For five years no books, only the poets and Shakespeare, and the notebooks and an expense account. . . . Jeffersonian democracy as an art is a thing to be desired. Let us by all means be artistic democrats.

Behold, I shall be a Caesar in the world of art, conquering every sort, every language and people, and lead their kings captive before the men of Rome. (Wow!)[10]

By January, 1905, however, he was still having difficulty drawing faces and figures and with making the most elementary sketches. Edgar Lee Masters quotes the following diary entry on a conversation with Robert Henri, who was one of Lindsay's art instructors at the Art Students League.

> Told me of the undiscovered mystery of the figure and face. Told me my faces were too doll-like, my figures lacked action. I ought to get same mystery in my face I did in my designs. Then ought to study Beardsley faces and figures. I believe Henri has the simplest way out for me.[11]

Lindsay's gifts, quite obviously, were not in realism, and his "mystery" was in his designs, where he hoped to unite drawing, poetry, and his visions. His first published work, in fact, was a drawing and poem used by the New York *Critic* in March, 1904, called "The Queen of Bubbles." And back in Springfield in the summer of 1904 more poems and visions came together in his initial drawing at that time of "The Map of the Universe." In later years he was to provide several explanations of the Map, and one should consult the ones in the 1925 edition of his *Collected Poems* and the 1925 issue of his *Village Magazine*, but the essential symbols were the same. The hero of Lindsay's Universe is Lucifer, who is not Satan but the "son of the morning" and King of Babylon punished in Isaiah 14. As Lindsay mythologized him in his early poem "The Last Song of Lucifer," this young singer was part Orpheus, part satanic rival of the existing order, and part Christian martyr. It was from hearing him sing to the demons of Hell that the angels left Heaven and became wandering martyrs too. Redemption of the Universe will come when the blood and tears of angels, saints, and other holy wanderers extinguish the flames of Hell and Laughing Bells (from the Tree of Laughing Bells in the West) come to every soul, satisfying "all memory, all hope, all borrowed sorrow."[12]

III

THE most commonly accepted explanation for Lindsay's walking tours is that he had not been able to publish poems and therefore decided to peddle them. It is just as true that by 1906 his attempt at supporting himself by his art had failed. In over four years in Chicago and New York he never sold a picture, never got the commissions for magazine illustrating and "cartooning" which he had expected, and never even won much encouragement or approval from his teachers. Stubborn idealism as well as lack of self-criticism prevented him from giving up. The turn did not come until one noontime in March, 1905, when he went to his art instructor, Robert Henri, and asked directly whether he ought to be a painter or a poet. There in the studio he recited "The Tree of Laughing Bells" with such effect that Henri, who of all his teachers had been most sympathetic, had no doubt. "I have a kind of pride about that moment," Henri told Lindsay twenty years later, "because I said to myself then, 'This fellow is a poet—he is a singer of songs.'" Lindsay's version was that Henri "certainly gave me a big brotherly boost."[13] From then on the drawing was secondary to the poetry.

His response was decisive, an anticipation of such similar endeavors of the 1950's and 60's as broadsides and leaflets of "penny poems." He had copies of two of his poems printed, and, according to his diaries, at 11 p.m. on March 23, 1905, headed down Tenth Avenue trying to sell them at bakeries, drug stores, fish markets, a Chinese laundry, and so on. He had been inspired by two things, the differences between them being quite characteristic of Lindsay: what he knew of the French troubadours, and President Roosevelt's method of bypassing his opposition by going directly to the voters. His earnings were only thirteen cents, but he was thrilled. He wrote in his diary:

> Now let there be here recorded my conclusions from one evening, one
> hour of peddling poetry. I am so rejoiced over it and so uplifted I am

going to do it many times. It sets the heart trembling with happiness. The people like poetry as well as the scholars, or better.[14]

During the next three weeks he made several more such excursions around Manhattan, including a final one through Hell's Kitchen on a Saturday night, and in them was obviously the basic idea of the begging tours. But the difference is that in New York he could only try to sell his poems—a poor business at 13¢ an hour—whereas in the country he could try to trade his poems, along with his skill in reciting them and entertaining people, for his board and lodging. In the country hospitality was easier, his visits would be a novelty, and he would look less like a pan-handler or freak. Finally, on Lindsay's intellectual horizon rural America was the real America, the "world behind the sky-scrapers," as he called it.

Keeping these other motives of Lindsay's in mind, I think we need to revise the oversimplified notion of the walks' purpose. Lindsay was neither a mere agrarian nor a nativist. On the contrary, it pained him that in America men of all races and nationalities were alienated from the achievements of their ancestors—the Irishman turned into the cop and the Italian into the fruit vendor. His own limited experience indicated, however, that it was principally the commercialized, competitive existence of large cities which forced people into these niches. He preferred to think (as Frederick Jackson Turner argued in the frontier thesis) that space gave men freedom, not only to develop themselves but to be known as themselves, unrestricted by prejudice and commerce. Furthermore, even at that date, America was still primarily a nation of farms and small towns, and other men as various as Woodrow Wilson and Josiah Royce were praising it for that and wishing it to remain that way. In a speech to the New Jersey Historical Society, Wilson had expressed a position very near to Lindsay's.

Local history is the ultimate substance of national history. There would be no epics were pastorals not also true,—no patriotism, were there no homes, no neighbors, no quiet round of civic duty; and I, for my part, do not wonder that scholarly men have been found not a few who, though they might have shone upon a larger field, where all eyes would have seen them win their fame, yet chose to pore all their lives long upon the blurred and scattered records of a country-side, where there was nothing but an old church or an ancient village. The history of a nation is only the history of its villages written large.[15]

Wilson's professorial eloquence is a long way from Lindsay's mixture of Middle Western drollery and fundamentalist fervor, but they share the Jeffersonian attachment to the village republic. The difference between Lindsay and the somewhat earlier regional local colorists (whom Wilson is in a sense speaking for) is that where they were nostalgic about the village, memorializing it in the face of industrialism and growing national uniformity, Lindsay was not thinking only of the past. He wanted to build it anew, make it over into the individualized thing it ought to be. In this respect, his position is stated better by Josiah Royce, who in a series of articles around the turn of the century, "Loyalty," "Provincialism," and others, advocated a strengthened provincial life as the essential counterweight to an industrial society's conformity and vanishing personal loyalties. This is the kind of planned regionalism later explained in much greater detail by Benton MacKaye, brother of Lindsay's fellow poet Percy MacKaye. It is primarily a sense that men prefer societies small enough and distinct enough that they can participate in them and identify their own character with the character of their own locale. Royce's model was Japan, a nation which he regarded as having industrialized extensively and yet not lost its various local manners and customs.

Lindsay's walks, therefore, were for a combination of reasons. That the official culture of the time would not buy his poems and art is true—even though Harriet Monroe may have later overemphasized this in order to dramatize the usefulness of her new magazine. But we should equally appreciate that the walks were an investigation of the quality of provincial life, a means of personal refreshment and renewal, and an application of Lindsay's religion of wandering martyrs. In the begging books Lindsay occasionally spoke of himself, in part humorously, as a St. Francis, but it is more to the point, I think, to recall his own singer Lucifer, "son of

22

the morning," who left his accustomed life and departed from established ways of singing in order to sing to the demons of hell, and whose example moved the saints angels to leave the "Jungles of Heaven." To describe the farmers and villagers who became Lindsay's hosts as "demons of hell" may not seem to fit very smoothly with the other elements of his vision (or with our patriotic sentimentality), but anyone reading his walk-books and his diaries carefully can readily see that these walks indeed did expose demons in the American landscape. The South, for example, had its gentlemanly old Confederate veterans discussing Poe and Burns, but it also had its feuding mountaineers and its incredibly racist freight train conductors. New Jersey and Pennsylvania had their friendly German farmers, but they also had the cruel and humiliating "missions" in Newark and Morristown and the dirty, suspicious railroad towns in the Susquehanna Valley.

Following the Southern walk in 1906, Lindsay stopped for a month with an aunt and uncle near Grassy Springs, Kentucky, and then went to Europe for the summer with his parents. In the fall he was back in New York, once more lecturing on art at the YMCA. One of his programs was a series of "fireside talks" on Sidney Lanier. Lindsay stood before the fire in the Y's living room, the lights out and a violinist playing! He wanted to lure in students just as the other night classes were ending and "send them home with sweet-flavored thoughts, so they will not be tempted before they get to their little hall bedrooms."[16] He also planned for the next walk, which he thought of making all the way from New York to Chicago. The new poem for it would be "God Help Us To Be Brave," a long inspirational piece celebrating his own world-pantheon of heroes, including Ramses II, Buddha, Shakespeare, Emerson, and Lincoln. The differences between this poem and "The Tree of Laughing Bells" recited in the South indicates the change in his intentions between the two walks. In the South he was simply presenting himself, and "The Tree" was from his inner universe. By 1908 he was campaigning, and the hero poem, despite its faults, was clearer and had greater popular appeal. It tried to put

greatness within reach of the common man, in a way leveling all
heroes by the broad catalogue, and giving the listener that inkling
of possibilities for himself which is the aim of so much American
inspirational literature. It was also incantatory, though it still
spoke in genteel phrases and did not have the revivalist vigor of his
later poems of this kind. This was to come only after four more
years back in Springfield and the much different experiences of the
1912 Western walk.

IV

TODAY the dominant view of the Populists comes surprising-
ly close to Matthew Arnold's school-masterish criticism of the
Romantics: they didn't know enough. What is emphasized is their
provinciality, the bigotry of their descendants, their refusal to develop farsighted programs and a disciplined political organization,
and their failure to reckon with the "inevitability" of industrial
power, urbanization, mass society, and the other almost insurmount-
able problems we feel beset us. To an indictment like this Lindsay
often seems as defenseless as his hero William Jennings Bryan.

And yet it is possible that the view itself is what is wrong—that
the view is an implicit confession of our own conservatism and
despair. We fail to keep in mind the basic fact that the Populists
were first and last idealistic democrats, whose ideal government is
really best described in Thoreau's definition of anarchy, "not the
absence of order but the absence of rule." Thus Populists would
restrain railroads, Wall Street, and the trusts because restraint was
necessary to protect the individual farmer, miner, or small merchant. Otherwise, a democracy of equals was impossible. And without equality, rule remained necessary, and the American order—
"the new order of the ages" or "novus ordo seclorum" still faith-
fully printed on dollar bills—remained impossible. Their goal was
not to solve the problems of mass society (which may, in fact, be
unsolvable), but to prevent them.

24

The basis of the order of equals, to Lindsay's line of Populists, has to be co-operation, mutual respect and affection, optimism, and good humor. Or, if these can be expressed in one word, the word to Lindsay was *beauty*. It seems almost archaic. However, to Lindsay and his contemporaries "beauty," as an ideal and as a civic goal, had two associations which may yet be familiar. First, he had in mind Ruskin and *The Stones of Venice*. Beauty could only be produced in a society which was itself beautiful, in its values, common aspirations, and civic forms and functions. And in such a society, beauty in art, architecture, and letters was an expression of the whole heart and soul of its creators and audience. Secondly, Lindsay had in mind the hopes and dreams of his own Middle Western America, where the raw, hasty, and unenhanced actuality somehow made numbers of the citizens long for "beauty" all the more. One manifestation of this is in the illustrations in late nineteenth-century county histories, where each mean or nondescript farm is represented with delicate fences, orderly yards, and neat shaded lanes. A later, more significant example was the City Beautiful movement, led by Louis Sullivan's one-time Chicago rival Daniel Burnham, which is probably most famous for reviving the L'Enfant plan for Washington, D.C., and getting the tracks of the Pennsylvania Railroad removed from the Capitol Mall. But the strength of such greater or lesser activities derived from both the desire for "beauty" and the fact that as a civic ideal "beauty" could engage the support of many men. By an application of Ruskin, one could argue that a Democracy ought to be the *most* beautiful society, if one thought, as the Populists surely did, that it had the highest modern social forms and values. Therefore, though Lindsay's Middle West wasn't beautiful, it held the faith that in time it would be, for the qualities of co-operation, mutual respect and affection, optimism, and good humor were its seeds.

The picture of Lindsay's unusual four years back in Springfield from 1908–12 given in his biographies is largely a bleak and angry one. Age 28 when he returned, age 32 when he left to begin the last walk, he still had no means of income and was dependent on his

25

parents. Such a man, who looked young and delicate, was not likely to be popular on Main Street. To make matters worse, he repeatedly hectored Main Street. Following a race riot in 1908, he gave a series of reproving lectures at the local YMCA on racial conflicts and stereotypes in America. In the summer of 1909 he began a private monthly called the *War Bulletin*.

> I have spent a great part of my few years fighting a soul battle for absolute liberty, for freedom from obligation, ease of conscience, independence from commercialism. I think I am farther from slavery than most men. But I have not complete freedom of speech. In my daily round of work I find myself taking counsel to please the stupid, the bigoted, the conservative, the impatient, the cheap. A good part of the time I can please these people, having a great deal in common with all of them—but—*the things that go into the War Bulletin please me only.*
> *To the Devil with you, average reader. To Gehenna with your stupidity, your bigotry, your conservatism, your cheapness and your impatience!*
> *In each new Bulletin the war shall go faster and further. War! War! War!*[17]

Thus separated from Springfield's proper citizens, Lindsay made other associations which may seem outlandish. Besides reading occasional prayers in Springfield's churches or speaking on Lincoln to groups of coal miners, for a considerable period he gave regular lectures for the Anti-Saloon League. His circuit was the tiny farm villages out on the edges of Sangamon County. He would ride out by train or interurban on Sunday mornings, and in the evenings speak at little frame churches. Yet this was not the simple Prohibitionism he was later to be accused of. What Lindsay found in mingling with the dry and godly farmers was a certain sense of community Springfield had lost. The proof is in an obscure contribution he made to a contest run by *Collier's* magazine in 1910 for letters on "The Church in Our Town." The contest had been provoked by a letter from a clergyman in Centerville, Massachusetts, who had argued that churches were declining in authority because they had become too loose in their membership and secular and socially oriented in their work. Lindsay, pointing to his experience in the hamlets of central Illinois, disagreed.

26

Just as such a place has white cement walks, holding it in one piece on the muddiest days, so it has its close corporation of the godly. Meeting houses dominate the landscape. Business is huddled away by the railroad station. The elect, who likewise represent the brains of the community, go the rounds of each other's amateur entertainments and returned-missionary-lectures. These people believe dancing a deed of shame, drinking a crime, card playing a step to hell. With an equal fervor they believe in the sacredness of the whole church activity. Who could call the elders stern who saw them sitting around the walls at the church socials smiling while the young folks played Jacob and Ruth, Drop the Handkerchief, Spin the Plate? Then kissing games are permitted at private parties, and moonlight drives to and from ice-cream suppers give range to satisfy all but the prodigal.[18]

The remainder of the short essay has the same tone. Lindsay is too tolerant himself to go along with the severities of this kind of "close corporation of the godly," but he is genuinely pleased by its community. The church, whatever its narrowness, was still a center of village life, dominating the landscape, keeping business in its place, and functioning day and night, seven days a week, to hold the village together, as strong a "cement" as the village walks. No wonder, then, that in *War Bulletin #2* he could fume against "conventional Christianity" until he sounded (as Edgar Lee Masters observed) like the old village atheist. Only the isolated village churches still played the organic community role he valued. And Lindsay is probably correct, our stereotypes to the contrary, that they performed the role with humor as well as severity, for the joy of the young as well as the piety of the "elect."

Even the *War Bulletin* usually had a kind of ostentatious fury and deliberate excess which should warn us from taking Lindsay's anger as "pure." Although it was infuriating to be called the town boob—and at times humiliating in that way only small towns can humiliate—Lindsay did not openly show his humiliation. He mocked, played with his detractors. *War Bulletin #4* came out in a different format, a notebook of poems called *The Tramp's Excuse*. Then at Christmas 1909, what might have been #6 was entitled *The Sangamon County Peace Advocate*, and even though he was now

27

thirty years old, he stood downtown on busy corners distributing it free to holiday shoppers. In it was "Springfield Magical," which attempted, with images from the *Arabian Nights*, to convey the city's unreality and mystery.

> In this, the City of my Discontent,
> Sometimes there comes a whisper from the grass,
> "Romance, Romance—is here. No Hindu town
> Is quite so strange. No Citadel of Brass
> By Sinbad found, held half such love and hate; . . ."

A more impersonal picture of Springfield at this period is to be found in *Social Conditions in an American City*, the results of a civic survey made in 1914 by a board of Springfield citizens with the support of the Russell Sage Foundation.[19] In population Springfield had grown from 34,159 in 1900 to 51,678 in 1910. 81% of its inhabitants were white native-born, 6% Negro, and 13% white foreign-born. For a Middle Western town it was somewhat unusual in being not only an agricultural and commercial center but also a center of railroads, manufacturing, and coal mining. Soot and fumes from the local soft coal filled the air and left a dark blue haze on windows. With approximately 9,000 homes in the city, there were approximately 7,000 fresh-water wells whose "pollution . . . is insured by 6,000 privy vaults." Houses of prostitution ("indicated by red lights, house names painted on the doors, and soliciting from windows"), dance halls, gambling parlors, and saloons all operated openly. Wages were very low. One half of the working men earned less than $10 a week, 70% of the working women less than $8 a week. (A prostitute, however, made an estimated $25 a week.) Child labor laws, though on the books, were not enforced. Springfield schools were old and badly designed and school recreational facilities were almost nil. One of the Survey's strongest recommendations was for all kinds of extensions in parks, playgrounds, and youth clubs. And yet in other sections of the city, Springfield must have looked very prosperous and smug—the face of that busy, merchants' Middle West then being eulogized by writers like Meredith Nicholson and Booth Tarkington. In those quar-

28

ters of town everybody had flush toilets and municipal water services; and there infant mortality was one-fourth what it was in the slums.

Needless to say, Lindsay's few allies were not from Springfield's comfortable upperclass. He kept company with a group of socialists and Swedenborgians held together by a woman named Maydie Lee, leader of the local chapter of the Women's Trade Union League. In the group were Mrs. Lee's brother Willis Spaulding, who was Commissioner of Public Property and a tireless agitator for a new water reservoir; Duncan McDonald, the secretary of the United Mine Workers of Illinois; Frank Bode, head of the Liberal Democrats; and a small number of dissident teachers, Knights of Columbus, Single Taxers, and a rabbi. It was a varied group, and such variety would have appealed to Lindsay as a proof of the general support reform programs might someday have. Lindsay also brought to it a small measure of outside encouragement, for he was slowly beginning to be published and was sending off his privately published manifestoes to every part of the country. "Subscribers" — voluntary and involuntary — to *The Village Magazine*, which he had printed in 1910, included Hamlin Garland, Witter Bynner, Marsden Hartley, William Marion Reedy, and Arthur Davison Ficke. In March, 1911, the New York periodical *Current Literature* carried a four-page article on the *Magazine*, with reproductions of six of Lindsay's illustrations.

Such activities help explain why when Lindsay commenced his last walk in late May, 1912, he left Springfield not simply as the poor artist-poet peddling his rhymes but as the bizarre evangelist "preaching the gospel of beauty." "The reason my beggar days started talk," he wrote later, "was that each time I broke loose, and went on the road, in the spring, after a winter of Art lecturing, it was definitely an act of protest against the United States commercial standard, a protest against the type of life set forth for all time in two books of Sinclair Lewis: *Babbitt* and *Main Street*."[20] As we have seen, this isn't the whole truth, but it does describe the frustration he must have felt after four years of fighting Main Street.

29

And yet he was going out to urge that other Main Streets redeem themselves.

His baggage, besides a toothbrush and a pocket handkerchief, consisted of copies of *Rhymes To Be Traded for Bread*; the pictures of "The Village Improvement Parade"; a scrapbook with pictures of temples and statues from around the world (the Parthenon, Taj Mahal, Trinity Church in New York) and pictures of his heroes (Lincoln, Tolstoy, Bryan, Buddha); and finally his leaflet proclaiming "The Gospel of Beauty." Explicitly the gospel said very little: only that craftsmen and artists should "wander over the whole nation in search of the secret of democratic beauty" and then return to labor in their native villages. It gives no hint of what the secret might be. What *are* democratic forms? What *will* be the provincial vernacular in American architecture, gardening, and park design? One reason why so many artists of Lindsay's generation did not return home was the very difficulty of these questions and the villagers' inability or unwillingness to face them seriously. And it can even be argued that Lindsay, presenting himself self-consciously as a "vain and foolish mendicant," did not take the questions entirely seriously either.

The other side of the argument is that Lindsay did apparently know his audience. The manner of Lindsay's pronouncement, with its pantheism, its exalting of hearth, democracy, and home town, could raise donations for the salvation of pirates in the Indian Ocean—like the King's camp-meeting appeal in *Huckleberry Finn*. This does not mean that Lindsay was humbugging his audience, however, but that he sought to enthrall and inspire first and then elaborate, if possible, later. It was an application of the populist (and Emersonian) principle that nothing great was ever done without enthusiasm. And the more serious elaboration of the "Gospel of Beauty" was in the three poems which he was prepared to recite under that title ("The Noble Farmer," "The Illinois Village," and "The Building of Springfield") and which he says in a note in his *Collected Poems* were the ones he did recite most often on this walk. They are an outline of the myths of the farmer, the village, and the town. The proud farmer "for a lifetime, saved the countryside," yet now the villagers watch the trains pass and want to leave. The town, therefore, must attract these creative children, forsake its materialism for parks and songs, and depend upon its own children to return and make "our dusty streets their goal. Within our attics hide their sacred tears." Here Lindsay was absolutely honest to the actualities of his own four-year experience. He was visionary and true. Ultimately, the building of Springfield can be done no other way. The "sacred tears" remind us both of the tears of the prophets and martyrs of Lindsay's "Map of the Universe" and also the tears this naive Lucifer himself must have shed in the upstairs of 603 South Fifth Street.

V

IN the preface to the 1925 edition of his *Collected Poems* Lindsay the famous "troubadour" wrote somewhat petulantly, "I want to be judged, not by my speaking tours, but by what I did before October, 1912, even before *Poetry Magazine* began, and before those tours began." It is a more sincere expression, perhaps, of his disgust with himself after that time than his disgust with his work. His own weakness for fame and flattery, mixed with his need of money, his uniqueness as a performer, and the hungry twentieth-century publicity machinery, had left him an exhausted man, the reciting freak. In addition, during the twenties Lindsay also succumbed on occasion to the nationalism and racism which was part of the decline of populism. Finally, after the death of his mother in 1922 and the renting of the old Springfield house, he was often a homeless man. For a little while he lived in Gulfport, Mississippi, teaching at a girls' junior college, and then in Spokane, Washington, where in 1925 he was married, at age 45. He tried, it appears, to imagine both Gulfport and Spokane as other Springfields, but he could not. It was not until the spring of 1929 that he was able to reclaim the Springfield house and move back with his wife and two children. Soon after came the Depression, with an inevitable falling off of the recital audiences which he now dreaded but depended on. Very early in the morning, December 5, 1931, he killed himself by drinking Lysol, the poisonous household disinfectant. He died in the room directly above the one in which he was born. His last words were, it is said, "I got them before they could get me — they can just try to explain this, if they can!"[21]

Lindsay's wish to be judged by what he did before 1912 does acknowledge that he had accomplished a great deal before the hour when fame reached him. All three of his walks, his best drawings, a substantial amount of his poetry, and the first issue of *The Village Magazine* were complete before then. Furthermore, many of his best poems, even though written after 1912, still commemorate incidents in his life or qualities in American culture which are from 1912 or before. This is not something critics have recognized, even the few good critics among the large band of mere adulators. Two of his best poems are the elegies to Lincoln and Altgeld, "Abraham Lincoln Walks at Midnight" and "The Eagle That Is Forgotten," which praise these leaders for an austere tranquility and a political bravery missing in a later time. Lindsay's other great leader was Bryan, whom he celebrated in a very different manner in the long "vaudeville" poem "Bryan, Bryan, Bryan, Bryan," but this poem too is retrospective. Its subtitle is "The Campaign of Eighteen Ninety-Six as Viewed at the Time by a Sixteen-Year-Old," and its raucous excitement recreates exactly the fervor of the Free Silver campaign and "Boy Bryan's" western admirers. It was written in Colorado in 1919, but only its mournful conclusion represented 1919.

Lindsay's poems deserve re-reading with this in mind. Randall Jarrell noted in 1962 that the Bryan poem had "a real aesthetic distance, an unexpected objectivity and historical truth that go along with the consciously exaggerated and audacious phrases."[22] But the same thing can also be said of several of the other great declamation pieces like "A Negro Sermon: Simon Legree," "Daniel," "The Kallyope Yell," and "The Santa-Fé Trail." In the case of the "Kallyope," the "futurism" is much closer to the revolu-

32

tionary futurism of Mayakovsky than to that of Marinetti, the writer of the "Futurist Manifesto" to whom Pound likened Lindsay. But once again, even his futurism is from his own point of view—the dream of industrial democracy as symbolized by the steam-organs and ice-cream stands at a turn-of-the-century carnival. And Lindsay's "Santa-Fé Trail" was based on his own lonely experience of that western highway in Kansas in 1912. He is not riding in the braying automobiles but standing along the highway's edge hearing them from way off in the distance. His Kansas is in the whispering cottonwoods and windmills and the faint song of the "Rachel-Jane" bird or Shivaree coming from the thorn bush at the end of the day. Very late in life, Lindsay's interests turned to the still more remote American past of Johnny Appleseed, Mohawks, and Buffaloes. From this concern there is one other poem which definitely merits attention, "The Flower-Fed Buffaloes."

It is obvious, then, that the 1912 walk was very important in Lindsay's career. It gave him material for poems, gave him an outlet for his "gospel of beauty," acquainted him with the vanishing populist Middle West of which Illinois had been only the eastern edge, and, finally, helped launch him on the dizzy course of popularity which was to have such a tragic end. Therefore, it makes sense that we should want to read the record of this walk as carefully as we can.

The record exists in both *Adventures While Preaching the Gospel of Beauty* and also Lindsay's unpublished diary. The diary was kept from day to day in a standard 6″ by 4″, leather-bound diary-book with a single page for each day of the year. The entries are not long, but since Lindsay wrote in a small and tight script, they do give a fairly detailed account of where he ate and slept and the things he had done and seen. However, two weeks after his arrival in Los Angeles in September (he had originally planned to walk all the way but had given up and taken the train from Wagon Mound, New Mexico, on September 13), this diary was lost, apparently forever. He had written his name and Springfield address in it, though, and in 1917 a woman living in Burbank, California, found it and mailed it to him, a valuable recovery but too late to

use in preparing *Adventures*. The book had been based on the
letters he had written to his parents and Octavia Roberts.

The first entry in the diary contained one very significant symbol
which is not mentioned in *Adventures*.

> Half way between Springfield and Jacksonville at about this hour in
> the afternoon I encountered by the side of the road Automobile 28058
> (Ill.) It was made in Moline, Illinois. It had been there in the ditch for
> days on account of a loss of ball-bearings in the front left wheel. The
> spider had built her nest within. The soft cushions were occupied by
> the beatle and the moth. The mud of many rains was upon her sides.
> Was the symbol and sign of my trip. All these goods and chariots have
> I discarded. They take to the ditch and confess themselves discom-
> fited before me.

Realistically, Lindsay is as mad as Quixote, and yet he also has a
strange Quixote-like grandeur. To have described the automobile's condition so carefully—and even written down its license
number—indicates that he regarded it like a casualty in some visionary tourney he had engaged it in. "They take to the ditch and
confess themselves discomfited before me." Here indeed was Lindsay as God's fool, the ageless boy so convinced by what he has set
out to do that reality somehow accommodated him.

The complementary moments to this one of romantic heroism
are the ones of pastoral tranquility and idealism. There was one
such moment on Friday, May 31 (*Adventures*, pp. 25–6) when
Lindsay happened up to an old-fashioned brick farmhouse, found
the doors unlocked and nobody home, and peered in through the
screens. The last sentence of the account in *Adventures*, "I went
away from that place," implies that he had been frightened by its
mystery and the probability of "a sleeping beauty somewhere
about!" But the account in the diary is a little different. "The roses
and pansies and geraniums were entrancing, and not a watch-dog
anywhere. The sleeping beauty must have been upstairs. I knocked
till I was tired and waited till I was tired, then bade the flowers
adieu. Ah, mysterious beautiful house." The house not only represented the Midwestern ideal of the prosperous, shaded farm

34

home, it also embodied deeper fantasies of the enchanted castle and the blessed (or cursed) damoiselle awaiting her errant knight. And Lindsay, though 32 years old, was still deeply enough a boy and dreamer to feel and succumb to such fantasies.

It is a fault, perhaps, of the published *Adventures* that they do not really contain enough of Lindsay's fantasy-life. The more grossly unrealistic examples, such as these two, are omitted or else chastened so as not to be offensive. What he generally plays up instead are his illusions of himself as tramp and happy wanderer, such as in the impulse to run for office on the tramp's program of having all railroad ties placed just the proper distance apart for walking. Lindsay seems to feel compelled to romanticize his tramp life in little ways like these possibly in order to fit the public taste for tramp books. But at the same time, he makes it very clear that he was not a *real* tramp, neither a Wobbly radical nor a full-time vagrant. His vagrant's motto is too pretty to be any real threat to the social order: "I am seeking the honey in labor, not the thorns." And consistent with his program or not, he is so genuinely pleased to stop with his parents' friend Professor Kerr in Emporia, Kansas, and rest and bathe that we are quite reassured that under the dirt and the suntan, he is still a middleclass gentleman. "Sooner or later," he realizes, "I am going to step up into the rarefied civilized air once too often and stay there in spite of myself." The remark was prophetic, and he also seems to have realized that even so, the polite world would be difficult for him.

The most extended sympathy with tramps Lindsay displays is in the short essay on wheat harvesters in chapter six, "The End of the Road." His epitaph to their life is clear enough, "The harvester, alas, is harvested." Since the farmers must hire him, the harvester can seek the highest possible wages by bargaining and moving around, but the gamblers, prostitutes, and police are waiting for him. Had Lindsay actually experienced it, he might have added that in some areas the farmers themselves combined to fix wages. But he was not making a social study, and although he was quite fascinated by this colorful and difficult life, he was also fundamen-

35

tally offended by its whole frantic, desperate, money-conscious nature. To him, the farmers, harvesters, and townspeople are all finally victims, all victims of a cruel system Lindsay intuitively resists. The irony, however, is at moments greater than he successfully conveys. Here is Kansas, his fair wonderland which he entered with images of wild strawberries and white New England churches, and the final story, if we omit the informal appendices, is the undertaker's tale of the field hand who left the field complaining of a headache and "fell dead by the roadside on the way to the house. He was face downward in an ant hill. He was eaten into an unrecognizable mass before they found him at sunset." And we have only the undertaker's sardonic American humor to console us: "The undertaker expatiated on how hard it was to embalm such folks."

In this perspective, it is easy to appreciate Lindsay's identification with "The Broncho That Would Not Be Broken" (as the poem was eventually entitled). Like Lindsay, it is young, untamed. It goes off to the fields "dancing." It resists getting in harness, and once harnessed is still devilish and unruly. For this it is mercilessly beaten by the farmers in charge of the reaping. Finally, with its many sores covered with flies and still no more obedient on the last day than the first, it is led away and dies lying on its back in the grass and kicking the air with its feet. Lindsay's reflections are that the broncho "should have been called Daniel Boone, or Davy Crockett or Custer or Richard, yes, Richard the Lion-Hearted." But the darkest similarity, in retrospect, is to Lindsay's own death, when he was beaten raw by creditors and by traveling and was scorned by editors and readers. Like the broncho (as well as the early American scouts and frontiersmen) Lindsay simply would not get in harness. Holding to his vision, even to its code of sacrifice and martyrdom, meant more to him than the American realities of wages and automobiles and selling one's self to the highest bidder. And he was not only ready to die for what he believed, he was prepared to be poor and disreputable for it too, which may be even more difficult for a famous American.

VI

LINDSAY'S populism, we can now see, informed his whole life. He filled his life with significant gestures which are frequently just as eloquent, or more eloquent, than his poetry and drawings. To be a populist artist to him meant seeking the "art-theory of the thoughts of the Declaration of Independence and Lincoln's Gettysburg Adress," but it also meant really living by those thoughts and by one's own example inspiring others to live that way too. This is challenging to the general modernist temper because it is the very opposite of the modernist principles that the artist should be disengaged from his work and that the reader should trust the poem, not the poet. Furthermore, re-appraising Lindsay today is all the harder because we are really no longer accustomed to finding the poet in the poems. We may think we do, but without knowing the man, we really aren't sure. And most often in Lindsay's case the poet is present not by his metaphors and images so much as by his voice. To see what this means, imagine the songs of Bob Dylan or other songs by the new wave of folk singers, *only* in print. Then imagine them read aloud, or even sung, but by somebody who can only make sense of them, not understand and interpret them correctly. These are problems the contemporary reader has with Lindsay, and they are not greatly alleviated by the availability today of the Caedmon recording of Lindsay reading. The poems read are few, the original recordings were 78 rpm's made in 1931, and Lindsay had recited most of the poems for so many years that he recited too rapidly and often very mechanically.[23]

Lindsay's life, therefore, is important in two ways. It is a guide to the poetry, and it is itself a major form of his expression. Moreover, it is reported by at least one of Lindsay's friends, the English journalist Stephen Graham, that Lindsay needed to be watched and lived with for awhile before one really had a very good idea what he might be trying to say. After meeting Lindsay in 1919, Graham had visited him in Springfield in 1921 and then gone hiking and climbing with him in Glacier National Park. Graham wrote up the experience in *Tramping with a Poet in the Rockies* and justified the book, in part, with the note that "despite his poetry, [Lindsay] is almost inarticulate." The book is valuable because Graham's English matter-of-factness was a good foil for Lindsay's flamboyance. Flamboyance, Lindsay explained, was his "protest against the drab, square-toed, dull, unimaginative America which is gaining on us all. . . . America simply *needs* the flamboyant to save her soul."

Democratic flamboyance may emanate from poets, but it cannot rely on poets alone. One of the most depressing things in the Lindsay history, after all, is the sense one repeatedly has that this was a man whose energy and nonconformity were constantly being used by the drabs and square-toes as a merely vicarious outlet without substance, a passive rebellion that merely listened and was entertained. And the more Lindsay felt this, the more he exhausted himself in trying to find new means of liberating them and new ways of shocking them. His incantatory poetry was like the revivalist minister's fiery sermon or the radical politician's oratory. The twenties did have their revivalists, but they were, as we know, badly lacking in authentic populist radicals, which makes it all the more interesting that Lindsay should have continually looked *back* to a time when populism was alive. As all his parades, proclamations, bulletins, broadsides and lectures amply show, Lindsay wanted *other* people to act as well.

It may be fitting, therefore, before concluding this essay to refer to two events in Springfield which were, in a small way, consequences of Lindsay's own hectoring and agitation. On a national level, of course, these events are infinitesimal, unless one sees them as symbolic of the kind of action other towns have also occasionally engaged in or unless one remembers that Springfield was Lindsay's lifelong burden and care.

The first event was the Springfield Exhibition of 1914, a follow-up of the popularly supported Springfield Survey already referred to. The idea of the Exhibition was to allow citizens who had taken part in the Survey or were disturbed by its findings the opportunity to acquaint the rest of the city with it and gain support for the reforms and improvements proposed. There were over 40 exhibit committees, which had spent two months in preparing the necessary posters, models, and displays; and the attendance, during the ten days the Exhibition was open in the fall of 1914, was over 15,000 people, more than a quarter of Springfield's population. Here were the dolls of "The Village Improvement Parade" actually moving, and Lindsay, to judge by his review of the exhibit in *The Survey*, the national magazine of this reform program, was charmed into a sense of wonder which made him quite tolerant of the naïveté of the performance.

> There was the ground plan in relief of the Enos school yard—laid out with much play-apparatus; the peep-show which showed the schoolroom empty at night, then filled with a social gathering; . . .Then there was the model-dairy-farm in miniature and the bad-farm. There was the photograph of the jail bull pen that lifted up and showed what was, perhaps, the most interesting peep-show of all, a picture of a farm where the man arrested was working out his penance, and perhaps his salvation, under human conditions—and a pretty little farm it was.

The second event was the opening of the Vachel Lindsay Bridge on July 12, 1935, which had been built to cross Lake Springfield, the addition to the city's water supply and park system which Lindsay's friend Willis Spaulding had advocated for years. Later in the summer the late poet received another tribute when a bust of Lindsay was unveiled at the Bridge's western end. Thus the prophet finally received some honor in his own city.

When that prophet, at the turning point of his life in 1913, had reconsidered the subject of vocation, his vision of himself as Lucifer was replaced by more sociable aims. "Every man has a social inclination," he wrote. "Mine is toward the field and I must live it out. . . .My horror is of the business office—and I have as much reason to reverence the instinct for labor as the instinct for art."

What more or in what different ways Lindsay might have contributed to American culture had he followed his humbler vision is a question. His immediate way of practicing it was "to preach in some country church on Sunday(s), like Grandpa Frazee," a plan which was not then absurd, for in 1913 the farmer-preacher had not yet vanished from American intellectual life. The idea of a poet's supporting himself by farming, at any rate, seemed at least persuasive enough to tempt Lindsay's equally unknown contemporary, Robert Frost. While Frost was no evangelist headed for the country pulpit, he did later discover a way of serving its successor, the country college. And the result was more than simply a pose. Carefully and personally defined, Frost's occupation as farmer-poet was a vantage point from which to make a regional pastoralism into a poetry very relevant to an urban age. The mordancy of New England rural speech and the psychic loneliness of hill farms spoke for much more than Vermont. In his own way, Lindsay might have also invented and transcended the old populist prairie towns. Instead, in so far as the prairie towns were created by literature at all, the job was done by novelists, who on the whole found more disillusion than wonder in them. Lindsay's wonder, which also could be bitterly critical, might have produced a vision very different from that of the novelists. There are hints of what it might have been, I think, in such poems as "Santa-Fé Trail," "Bryan, Bryan, Bryan, Bryan," "Eagle Forgotten," and "The Flower-Fed Buffaloes." To the contemporary ear, there may still be too many echoes of patriotic "declamation" in Lindsay and thus too many thoughts of the defeated promise which he himself knew. But that being the case, what value is in Lindsay will become clear once again if and when the promise of this nation becomes clearer. Promise and wonder go together, and Vachel Lindsay was well endowed with both.

40

NOTES

1. Harriet Monroe, *A Poet's Life* (New York: The Macmillan Co., 1938), p. 279.

2. *Ibid.*, p. 337.

3. "Sincerity in the Making," *The New Republic*, 1 (December 5, 1914), 26.

4. *Letters of Nicholas Vachel Lindsay to A. Joseph Armstrong*, ed. A. Joseph Armstrong (Waco, Texas: Baylor Univ. Press, 1940), p. 90.

5. D. D. Paige (ed.), *The Letters of Ezra Pound, 1907–1941* (London: Faber & Faber, 1951), pp. 92, 99, 101, 109.

6. Eleanor Ruggles, *The West-Going Heart: A Life of Vachel Lindsay* (New York: W. W. Norton & Co., 1959), p. 176.

7. For permission to consult and quote from Lindsay's diaries of his walking tours I am indebted to the Clifton Waller Barrett Collection at the Alderman Library, the University of Virginia. I would also like to acknowledge my debts to Mr. Nicholas C. Lindsay, his father's literary executor, for permissions and many kinds of assistance; to my colleague Sherman Paul, who read an early version of this essay; and to the University of Iowa Graduate College for microfilms of the diaries.

8. Edgar Lee Masters, *Vachel Lindsay: A Poet in America* (New York: Charles Scribner's Sons, 1935); Mark Harris, *City of Discontent* (Indianapolis: Bobbs-Merrill Co., 1952); and Eleanor Ruggles, *op. cit.* My synopsis of Lindsay's life draws chiefly on Masters and Ruggles.

9. *An Autobiographical Novel* (Garden City, N.Y.: Doubleday & Co., 1966), p. 27.

10. Quoted in Masters, p. 105.

11. Masters, p. 120.

12. Vachel Lindsay, *The Village Magazine* (Springfield, Ill., 1925), p. 168.

13. Ruggles, pp. 93–4; Masters, p. 120.

14. Ruggles, p. 97.

15. "The Course of American History," *Mere Literature and Other Essays* (Boston: Houghton Mifflin Co., 1896), pp. 213–4.

16. Ruggles, p. 125.

17. Ruggles, p. 145.

18. "The Factor in the Village," *Colliers*, XLV (August 13, 1910), p. 30.

19. Shelby M. Harrison, *Social Conditions in an American City: A Summary of the Findings of the Springfield Survey* (New York: Russell Sage Foundation, 1920).

20. Vachel Lindsay, *Collected Poems* (New York: Macmillan Co., 1925), p. 19.

21. Ruggles, p. 432. Masters, p. 361: "They tried to get me; I got them first."

22. "Fifty Years of American Poetry," *National Poetry Festival* (Washington, D.C.: The Library of Congress, 1963), p. 116.

23. The re-issue of the old records also leaves out several of the major poems recorded, notably "Santa-Fé Trail," which was played for me in September, 1965, by Miss Elizabeth Graham, custodian of the Lindsay House in Springfield. It was Miss Graham, who in the course of many informative remarks on Lindsay explained the defects of the recordings made in 1931 at Columbia University for the National Council of Teachers of English. Recently, Nicholas Lindsay has recorded some of his own readings of his father's poems (Caedmon TC 1216), which are excellent.

41

Adventures while Preaching
The Gospel of Beauty

by

NICHOLAS VACHEL LINDSAY

In the summer of 1912 Mr. Lindsay walked from his home town, Springfield, through Missouri and Kansas, up and down Colorado and into New Mexico. His rules were "to have nothing to do with cities, railroad money, baggage or fellow-tramps. Such wages as I made I sent home, starting out broke again, spending just enough for one day's recuperation out of each pile. . . I always walked penniless. My baggage was practically nil."

For his board and lodging, when he didn't help harvest, he offered "Rhymes to Be Traded For Bread" with the Gospel of Beauty that it contained.

And this new book is simply Mr. Lindsay's story of that extraordinary walk with an account of the various adventures that befell him and with a number of charming poems interspersed.

MITCHELL KENNERLEY **PUBLISHER NEW YORK**

Original jacket front

ABOUT THE AUTHOR

Nicholas Vachel Lindsay is best known perhaps for his poem "General William Booth Enters into Heaven" published last year by Mitchell Kennerley, but written in Los Angeles, October 1912.

Mr. Lindsay was born in the house where he now lives in Springfield, Illinois, November tenth 1879. At the Springfield High School, he was Champion Walker. In 1897 he began to write poems and illustrate them at the same time He spent three years at Hiram College and from 1900-1903 studied at the Chicago art Institute. The next winter he spent at the New York School of Art under Chase and Henri. Meanwhile many of his poems found their way into print.

He lectured nights at the Y. M. C. A in New York and in the Spring of 1906 went on his first long tramp, begging his way through Florida, Georgia, North Carolina, Tennessee and Kentucky. This was followed by a trip to Europe where he studied thoroughly some twenty museums. Returning home, he resumed his lecturing but late in 1908 he left New York for good and has ever since been a Springfield citizen. He worked for the Anti-Saloon League of Illinois-and "discovered" the farmers whom he regards as the people most worth while.

From time to time Mr. Lindsay has printed works of his in prose and verse for free distribution--- sometimes to be used for exchange for board and lodging. Among these may be mentioned half a dozen so-called "War Bulletins," "The Village Magazine" and "Rhymes To Be Traded For Bread "

On May 27th, 1912 Mr. Lindsay started the walk recorded in this new book. Since then he has been much in the public eye.

For the benefit of those who mispronounce his name Mr. Lindsay has written the following amusing couplets.

My middle name rhymes not with satchel,
So please do not pronounce it "Vatchell"
My middle name rhymes not with Rock Hell
So please do not pronounce it "Vock Hell"
My middle name rhymes not with Hasb Hell
So please do not pronounce it "Vasch Hell"
My middle name rhymes not with Bottle
So please do not pronounce it "Vottle"
My name is just the same as Rachel
With V for R.
Please call me Vachel

Original jacket flap

Adventures While Preaching the Gospel of Beauty

I

I Start on My Walk

AS some of the readers of this account are aware, I took a walk last summer from my home town, Springfield, Illinois, across Illinois, Missouri, and Kansas, up and down Colorado and into New Mexico. One of the most vivid little episodes of the trip, that came after two months of walking, I would like to tell at this point. It was in southern Colorado. It was early morning. Around the cliff, with a boom, a rattle and a bang, appeared a gypsy wagon. On the front seat was a Romany, himself dressed inconspicuously, but with his woman more bedecked than Carmen. She wore the bangles and spangles of her Hindu progenitors. The woman began to shout at me, I could not distinguish just what. The two seemed to think this was the gayest morning the sun ever shone upon. They came faster and faster, then, suddenly, at the woman's suggestion, pulled up short. And she asked me with a fraternal, confidential air, "What you sellin', what you sellin', boy?"

If we had met on the first of June, when I had just started, she would have pretended to know all about me, she would have asked to tell my fortune. On the first of June I wore about the same costume I wear on the streets of Springfield. I was white as paper from two years of writing poetry indoors. Now, on the first of August I was sunburned a quarter of an inch deep. My costume, once so respectable, I had gradually transformed till it looked like that of a showman. I wore very yellow corduroys, a fancy sombrero and an oriflamme tie. So Mrs.

I START ON MY WALK

Gypsy hailed me as a brother. She eyed my little worn-out oil-cloth pack. It was a delightful professional mystery to her.

I handed up a sample of what it contained —my *Gospel of Beauty* (a little one-page formula for making America lovelier), and my little booklet, *Rhymes to Be Traded for Bread.*

The impatient horses went charging on. In an instant came more noises. Four more happy gypsy wagons passed. Each time the interview was repeated in identical language, and with the same stage business. The men were so silent and masterful-looking, the girls such brilliant, inquisitive cats! I never before saw anything so like high-class comic opera off the stage, and in fancy I still see it all:—those brown, braceleted arms still waving, and those provocative siren cries:—"What you sellin', boy? What you sellin'?"

I hope my Gospel did them good. Its essential principle is that one should not be

a gypsy forever. He should return home.
Having returned, he should plant the seeds
of Art and of Beauty. He should tend them
till they grow. There is something essentially humorous about a man walking rapidly away from his home town to tell all men
they should go back to their birthplaces. It
is still more humorous that, when I finally
did return home, it was sooner than I intended, all through a temporary loss of
nerve. But once home I have taken my own
advice to heart. I have addressed four
mothers' clubs, one literary club, two missionary societies and one High School De-
bating Society upon the Gospel of Beauty.
And the end is not yet. No, not by any
means. As John Paul Jones once said, "I
have not yet begun to fight."

I had set certain rules of travel, evolved
and proved practicable in previous expe-
ditions in the East and South. These rules
had been published in various periodicals before my start. The home town newspapers,

my puzzled but faithful friends in good times and in bad, went the magazines one better and added a rule or so. To promote the gala character of the occasion, a certain paper announced that I was to walk in a Roman toga with bare feet encased in sandals. Another added that I had travelled through most of the countries of Europe in this manner. It made delightful reading. Scores of mere acquaintances crossed the street to shake hands with me on the strength of it.

The actual rules were to have nothing to do with cities, railroads, money, baggage or fellow tramps. I was to begin to ask for dinner about a quarter of eleven and for supper, lodging and breakfast about a quarter of five. I was to be neat, truthful, civil and on the square. I was to preach the Gospel of Beauty. How did these rules work out?

The cities were easy to let alone. I passed quickly through Hannibal and Jefferson City. Then, straight West, it was nothing but villages and farms till the three main cities of Colorado. Then nothing but desert to central New Mexico. I did not take the train till I reached central New Mexico, nor did I write to Springfield for money till I quit the whole game at that point.

Such wages as I made I sent home, starting out broke again, first spending just enough for one day's recuperation out of each pile, and, in the first case, rehabilitating my costume considerably. I always walked penniless. My baggage was practically nil. It was mainly printed matter, renewed by mail. Sometimes I carried reproductions of drawings of mine, *The Village Improvement Parade,* a series of picture-cartoons with many morals.

I pinned this on the farmers' walls, explaining the mottoes on the banners, and exhorting them to study it at their leisure. My little pack had a supply of the aforesaid

I START ON MY WALK

Rhymes to Be Traded for Bread. And it contained the following Gospel of Beauty:

THE GOSPEL OF BEAUTY

Being the new "creed of a beggar" by that vain and foolish mendicant Nicholas Vachel Lindsay, printed for his personal friends in his home village—Springfield, Illinois. It is his intention to carry this gospel across the country beginning June, 1912, returning in due time.

I

I come to you penniless and afoot, to bring a message. I am starting a new religious idea. The idea does not say "no" to any creed that you have heard. . . . After this, let the denomination to which you now belong be called in your heart "the church of beauty" or "the church of the open sky." . . . The church of beauty has two sides: the love of beauty and the love of God.

THE GOSPEL OF BEAUTY

II

THE NEW LOCALISM

The things most worth while are one's own hearth and neighborhood. We should make our own home and neighborhood the most democratic, the most beautiful and the holiest in the world. The children now growing up should become devout gardeners or architects or park architects or teachers of dancing in the Greek spirit or musicians or novelists or poets or story-writers or craftsmen or wood-carvers or dramatists or actors or singers. They should find their talent and nurse it industriously. They should believe in every possible application to art-theory of the thoughts of the Declaration of Independence and Lincoln's Gettysburg Address. They should, if led by the spirit, wander over the whole nation in search of the secret of democratic beauty with their hearts at the same time filled to overflowing with the righteousness of God. Then they should come back to their own hearth and neighborhood and gather a little circle of their own sort of workers about them and strive to make the neighborhood and home more beautiful and democratic and holy with their special art. . . . They should labor in their little circle expecting neither reward nor honors. . . . In their darkest hours they should be made strong by the vision of a completely beautiful neighborhood and the passion for a completely democratic art. Their reason for living should be that joy in beauty which no wounds can take away, and that joy in the love of God which no crucifixion can end.

The kindly reader at this point clutches his brow and asks, "But why carry this paper around? Why, in Heaven's name, do it as a beggar? Why do it at all?"

Let me make haste to say that there has

been as yet no accredited, accepted way for establishing Beauty in the heart of the average American. *Until such a way has been determined upon by a competent committee, I must be pardoned for taking my own course and trying any experiment I please.*

But I hope to justify the space occupied by this narrative, not by the essential seriousness of my intentions, nor the essential solemnity of my motley cloak, nor by the final failure or success of the trip, but by the things I unexpectedly ran into, as curious to me as to the gentle and sheltered reader. Of all that I saw the State of Kansas impressed me most, and the letters home I have chosen cover, for the most part, adventures there.

Kansas, the Ideal American Community! Kansas, nearer than any other to the kind of a land our fathers took for granted! Kansas, practically free from cities and industrialism, the real last refuge of the constitution, since it maintains the type of agricultural civilization the constitution had in mind! Kansas, State of tremendous crops and hardy, devout, natural men! Kansas of the historic Santa Fé Trail and the classic village of Emporia and the immortal editor of Emporia! Kansas, laid out in roads a mile apart, criss-crossing to make a great checker-board, roads that go on and on past endless rich farms and big farm-houses, though there is not a village or railroad for miles! Kansas, the land of the real country gentlemen, Americans who work the soil and own the soil they work; State where the shabby tenant-dwelling scarce appears as yet! Kansas of the Chautauqua and the college student and the devout school-teacher! The dry State, the automobile State, the insurgent State! Kansas, that is ruled by the cross-roads church, and the church type of civilization! The Newest New England! State of more promise of permanent spiritual glory than Massachusetts in her brilliant youth!

THE GOSPEL OF BEAUTY

Travellers who go through in cars with roofs know little of this State. Kansas is not Kansas till we march day after day, away from the sunrise, under the blistering noon sky, on, on over a straight west-going road toward the sunset. Then we begin to have our spirits stirred by the sight of the tremendous clouds looming over the most interminable plain that ever expanded and made glorious the heart of Man.

I have walked in eastern Kansas where the hedged fields and the orchards and gardens reminded one of the picturesque sections of Indiana, of antique and settled Ohio. Later I have mounted a little hill on what was otherwise a level and seemingly uninhabited universe, and traced, away to the left, the creeping Arkansas, its course marked by the cottonwoods, that became like tufts of grass on its far borders. All the rest of the world was treeless and riverless, yet green from the rain of yesterday, and patterned like a carpet with the shadows of the clouds. I have walked on and on across this unbroken prairie-sod where half-wild cattle grazed. Later I have marched between alfalfa fields where hovered the lavender haze of the fragrant blossom, and have heard the busy music of the gorging bumble bees. Later I have marched for days and days with wheat waving round me, yellow as the sun. Many's the night I have slept in the barn-lofts of Kansas with the wide loft-door rolled open and the inconsequential golden moon for my friend.

These selections from letters home tell how I came into Kansas and how I adventured there. The letters were written avowedly as a sort of diary of the trip, but their contents turned out to be something less than that, something more than that, and something rather different.

THURSDAY, MAY 30, 1912. In the blue grass by the side of the road. Somewhere west of Jacksonville, Illinois. Hot sun.

Cool wind.   Rabbits in the distance.   Bumblebees near.

At five last evening I sighted my lodging for the night.   It was the other side of a high worm fence.   It was down in the hollow of a grove.   It was the box of an old box-car, brought there somehow, without its wheels.   It was far from a railroad.   I said in my heart "Here is the appointed shelter." I was not mistaken.

As was subsequently revealed, it belonged to the old gentleman I spied through the window stemming gooseberries and singing: "John Brown's body."   He puts the car top on wagon wheels and hauls it from grove to grove between Jacksonville and the east bank of the Mississippi.   He carries a saw mill equipment along.   He is clearing this wood for the owner, of all but its walnut trees.   He lives in the box with his son and two assistants.   He is cook, washerwoman and saw-mill boss.   His wife died many years ago.

I START ON MY WALK

The old gentleman let me in with alacrity. He allowed me to stem gooseberries while he made a great supper for the boys. They soon came in. I was meanwhile assured that my name was going into the pot. My host looked like his old general, McClellan. He was eloquent on the sins of preachers, dry voters and pension reformers. He was full of reminiscences of the string band at Sherman's headquarters, in which he learned to perfect himself on his wonderful fiddle. He said, "I can't play slow music. I've got to play dance tunes or die." He did not die. His son took a banjo from an old trunk and the two of them gave us every worth while tune on earth: *Money Musk, Hell's Broke Loose in Georgia, The Year of Jubilee, Sailor's Hornpipe, Baby on the Block, Lady on the Lake,* and *The Irish Washerwoman,* while I stemmed gooseberries, which they protested I did not need to do. Then I read my own unworthy verses to the romantic and violin-stirred

THE GOSPEL OF BEAUTY

company. And there was room for all of us to sleep in that one repentant and converted box-car.

FRIDAY, MAY 31, 1912. Half an hour after a dinner of crackers, cheese and raisins, provided at my solicitation by the grocer in the general store and post-office, Valley City, Illinois.

I have thought of a new way of stating my economic position. I belong to one of the leisure classes, that of the rhymers. In order to belong to any leisure class, one must be a thief or a beggar. On the whole I prefer to be a beggar, and, before each meal, receive from toiling man new permission to extend my holiday. The great business of that world that looms above the workshop and the furrow is to take things from people by some sort of taxation or tariff or special privilege. But I want to exercise my covetousness only in a retail way, open and above board, and when I take bread from a man's table I want to ask him for that particular piece of bread, as politely as I can.

But this does not absolutely fit my life. For yesterday I ate several things without permission, for instance, in mid-morning I devoured all the cherries a man can hold. They were hanging from heavy, breaking branches that came way over the stone wall into the road.

Another adventure. Early in the afternoon I found a brick farmhouse. It had a noble porch. There were marks of old-fashioned distinction in the trimmed hedges and flower-beds, and in the summer-houses. The side-yard and barn-lot were the cluckingest, buzzingest kind of places. There was not a human being in sight. I knocked and knocked on the doors. I wandered through all the sheds. I could look in through the unlocked screens and see every sign of present occupation. If I had chosen to enter I could have stolen the wash bowl or the baby-buggy or the baby's doll. The creamery was more tempting, with milk and butter and eggs, and freshly pulled taffy cut in squares. I took a little taffy. That is all I took, though the chickens were very social and I could have eloped with several of them. The roses and peonies and geraniums were entrancing, and there was not a watch dog anywhere. Everything seemed to say *"Enter in and possess!"*

I saw inside the last door where I knocked a crisp, sweet, simple dress on a chair. Ah, a sleeping beauty somewhere about!

I went away from that place.

SUNDAY, JUNE 1, 1912. By the side of the road, somewhere in Illinois.

Last night I was dead tired. I hailed a man by the shed of a stationary engine. I asked him if I could sleep in the engine-shed all night, beginning right now. He said "Yes." But from five to six, he put me out of doors, on a pile of gunny sacks on the grass. There I slept while the ducks quacked in my ears, and the autos whizzed over the bridge three feet away. My host was a one-legged man. In about an hour he came poking me with that crutch and that peg of his. He said "Come, and let me tell your fortune! I have been studying your physiognifry while you were asleep!" So we sat on a log by the edge of the pond. He said: "I am the Seventh Son of a Seventh Son. They call me the duck-pond diviner. I forecast the weather for these parts. Every Sunday I have my corner for the week's weather in the paper here." Then he indulged in a good deal of the kind of talk one finds in the front of the almanac.

He was a little round man with a pair of round, dull eyes, and a dull, round face, with a two weeks' beard upon it. He squinted up his eyes now. He was deliberate. Switch engines were going by. He paused to hail the engineers. Here is a part of what he finally said: "You are a Child of Destiny." He hesitated, for he wanted to be sure of the next point. "You were born in the month of S-e-p-t-e-m-b-e-r. Your preference is for a business like clerking in a store. You are of a slow, *pigmatic* temperament, but I can see you are fastidious about your eating. You do not use tobacco. You are fond of sweets. You have been married twice. Your first wife died, and your second was divorced. You look like you would make a good spiritualist medium. If you don't let any black cats cross your track you will have good luck for the next three years."

He hit it right twice. I *am* a Child of Destiny and I *am* fond of sweets. When a prophet hits it right on essentials like that, who would be critical?

An old woman with a pipe in her mouth came down the railroad embankment looking for greens. He bawled at her "Git out of that." But on she came. When she was closer he said: "Them weeds is full of poison oak." She grunted, and kept working her way toward us, and with a belligerent swagger marched past us on into the engine-room, carrying a great mess of greens in her muddy hands.

There was scarcely space in that little shed for the engine, and it was sticking out in several places. Yet it dawned on me that this was the wife of my host, that they kept house with that engine for the principal article of furniture. Without a word of introduction or explanation she stood behind me and mumbled, "You need your supper, son. Come in."

There was actually a side-room in that little box, a side room with a cot and a cupboard as well. On the floor was what was once a rug. But it had had a long kitchen history. She dipped a little unwashed bowl into a larger unwashed bowl, with an unwashed thumb doing its whole duty. She handed me a fuzzy, unwashed spoon and said with a note of real kindness, "Eat your supper, young man." She patted me on the shoulder with a sticky hand. Then she stood, looking at me fixedly. The woman had only half her wits.

I suppose they kept that stew till it was used up, and then made another. I was a Child of Destiny, all right, and Destiny decreed I should eat. I sat there trying to think of things to say to make agreeable conversation, and postpone the inevitable. Finally I told her I wanted to be a little boy once more, and take my bowl and eat on the log by the pond in the presence of Nature.

She maintained that genial silence which indicates a motherly sympathy. I left her smoking and smiling there. And like a little child that knows not the folly of waste, I slyly fed my supper to the ducks.

At bedtime the old gentleman slept in his clothes on the cot in the kitchenette. He had the dog for a foot-warmer. There was a jar of yeast under the table. Every so often the old gentleman would call for the old lady to come and drive the ducks out, or they would get the board off the jar. Ever and anon the ducks had a taste before the avenger arrived.

On one side of the engine the old lady had piled gunny-sacks for my bed. That softened the cement-floor foundation. Then she insisted on adding that elegant rug from the kitchen, to protect me from the fuzz on the sacks. She herself slept on a pile of excelsior with a bit of canvas atop. She kept a cat just by her cheek to keep her warm, and I have no doubt the pretty brute whispered things in her ear. Tabby was the one aristocratic, magical touch:—one of these golden coon-cats.

The old lady's bed was on the floor, just around the corner from me, on the other side of the engine. That engine stretched its vast bulk between us. It was as the sword between the duke and the queen in the fairy story. But every so often, in response to the old gentleman's alarm, the queen would come climbing over my feet in order to get to the kitchen and drive out the ducks. From where I lay I could see through two doors to the night outside. I could watch the stealthy approach of the white and waddling marauders. Do not tell me a duck has no sense of humor. It was a great game of tag to them. It occurred as regularly as the half hours were reached. I could time the whole process by the ticking in my soul, while presumably asleep. And while waiting for them to come up I could see the pond and a star reflected in the pond, the star of my Destiny, no doubt. At last it began to rain. Despite considerations of fresh air, the door was shut, and soon everybody was asleep.

The bed was not verminiferous. I dislike all jokes on such a theme, but in this case the issue must be met. It is the one thing the tramp wants to know about his bunk. That peril avoided, there is nothing to quarrel about. Despite all the grotesquerie of that night, I am grateful for a roof, and two gentle friends.

Poor things! Just like all the citizens of the twentieth century, petting and grooming machinery three times as smart as they are themselves. Such people should have engines to take care of them, instead of taking care of engines. There stood the sleek brute in its stall, absorbing all, giving nothing, pumping supplies only for its own caste;— water to be fed to other engines.

But seldom are keepers of engine-stables as unfortunate as these. The best they can get from the world is cruel laughter. Yet this woman, crippled in brain, her soul only half alive, this dull man, crippled in body, had God's gift of the liberal heart. If they are supremely absurd, so are all of us. We must include ourselves in the farce. These two, tottering through the dimness and vexation of our queer world, were willing the stranger should lean upon them. I say they had the good gift of the liberal heart. One

THE GOSPEL OF BEAUTY

thing was theirs to divide. That was a roof. They gave me my third and they helped me to hide from the rain. In the name of St. Francis I laid me down. May that saint of all saints be with them, and with all the gentle and innocent and weary and broken!

UPON RETURNING TO THE COUNTRY ROAD

Even the shrewd and bitter,
Gnarled by the old world's greed,
Cherished the stranger softly
Seeing his utter need.
Shelter and patient hearing,
These were their gifts to him,
To the minstrel chanting, begging,
As the sunset-fire grew dim.
The rich said "You are welcome."

Yea, even the rich were good.
How strange that in their feasting
His songs were understood!
The doors of the poor were open,
The poor who had wandered too,
Who had slept with ne'er a roof-tree

I START ON MY WALK

Under the wind and dew.
The minds of the poor were open,
There dark mistrust was dead.
They loved his wizard stories,
They bought his rhymes with bread.

Those were his days of glory,
Of faith in his fellow-men.
Therefore, to-day the singer
Turns beggar once again.

II

Walking Through Missouri

TUESDAY MORNING, JUNE 4, 1912. In a hotel bedroom in Laddonia, Missouri. I occupy this room without charge.

Through the mercy of the gateman I crossed the Hannibal toll-bridge without paying fare, and the more enjoyed the pearly Mississippi in the evening twilight. Walking south of Hannibal next morning, Sunday, I was irresistibly reminded of Kentucky. It was the first real "pike" of my journey,—solid gravel, and everyone was exercising his racing pony in his racing cart, and giving me a ride down lovely avenues of trees. Here, as in dozens of other interesting "lifts" in Illinois, I had the driver's complete attention, recited *The Gospel of*

Beauty through a series of my more didactic rhymes till I was tired, and presented the *Village Improvement Parade* and the *Rhymes to Be Traded for Bread* and exhorted the comradely driver to forget me never. One colored horseman hitched forward on the plank of his breaking-cart and gave me his seat. Then came quite a ride into New London. He asked, "So you goin' to walk west to the mountains and all around?" "Yes, if this colt don't break my neck, or I don't lose my nerve or get bitten by a dog or anything." "Will you walk back?" "Maybe so, maybe not." He pondered a while, then said, with the Bert Williams manner, *"You'll ride back. Mark my words, you'll ride back!"*

He asked a little later, "Goin' to harves' in Kansas?" I assured him I was not going to harvest in Kansas. He rolled his big white eyes at me: "What in the name of Uncle Hillbilly *air* you up to then?"

In this case I could not present my tracts,

for I was holding on to him for dear life. Just then he turned off my road. Getting out of the cart I nearly hung myself; and the colt was away again before I could say "Thank you."

Yesterday I passed through what was mostly a flat prairie country, abounding in the Missouri mule. I met one man on horseback driving before him an enormous specimen tied head to head with a draught-horse. The mule was continually dragging his good-natured comrade into the ditch and being jerked out again. The mule is a perpetual inquisitor and experimenter. He followed me along the fence with the alertest curiosity, when he was inside the field, yet meeting me in the road, he often showed deadly terror. If he was a mule colt, following his mare mamma along the pike, I had to stand in the side lane or hide behind a tree till he went by, or else he would turn and run as if the very devil were after him. Then the farmer on the mare would have to pursue him a considerable distance, and drive him back with cuss words. 'Tis sweet to stir up so much emotion, even in the breast of an animal.

What do you suppose happened in New London? I approached what I thought a tiny Baptist chapel of whitewashed stone. Noting it was about sermon-time, and feeling like repenting, I walked in. Behold, the most harmoniously-colored Catholic shrine in the world! The sermon was being preached by the most gorgeously robed priest one could well conceive. The father went on to show how a vision of the Christ-child had appeared on the altar of a lax congregation in Spain. From that time those people, stricken with reverence and godly fear, put that church into repair, and the community became a true servant of the Lord. Infidels were converted, heretics were confounded.

After the sermon came the climax of the mass, and from the choir loft above my head came the most passionate religious singing I ever heard in my life. The excellence of the whole worship, even to the preaching of visions, was a beautiful surprise.

People do not open their eyes enough, neither their spiritual nor their physical eyes. They are not sensitive enough to loveliness either visible or by the pathway of visions. I wish every church in the world could see the Christ-child on the altar, every Methodist and Baptist as well as every Catholic congregation.

With these thoughts I sat and listened while that woman soloist sang not only through the Mass, but the Benediction of the Blessed Sacrament as well. The whole surprise stands out like a blazing star in my memory.

I say we do not see enough visions. I wish that, going out of the church door at noon, every worshipper in America could spiritually discern the Good St. Francis come down to our earth and singing of the

Sun. I wish that saint would return. I wish he would preach voluntary poverty to all the middle-class and wealthy folk of this land, with the power that once shook Europe.

FRIDAY, JUNE 7, 1912. In the mid-afternoon in the woods, many miles west of Jefferson City. I am sitting by a wild rose bush. I am looking down a long sunlit vista of trees.

Wednesday evening, three miles from Fulton, Missouri, I encountered a terrific storm. I tried one farm-house just before the rain came down, but they would not let me in, not even into the barn. They said it was "not convenient." They said there was another place a little piece ahead, anyway. Pretty soon I was considerably rained upon. But the "other place" did not appear. Later the thunder and lightning were frightful. It seemed to me everything was being struck all around me: because of the sheer downpour it became pitch dark. It seemed as though the very weight of the rain would beat me into the ground. Yet I felt that I needed the washing. The night before I enjoyed the kind of hospitality that makes one yearn for a bath.

At last I saw a light ahead. I walked through more cataracts and reached it. Then I knocked at the door. I entered what revealed itself to be a negro cabin. Mine host was Uncle Remus himself, only a person of more delicacy and dignity. He appeared to be well preserved, though he was eighteen years old when the war broke out. He owns forty acres and more than one mule. His house was sweet and clean, all metal surfaces polished, all wood-work scrubbed white, all linen fresh laundered. He urged me to dry at his oven. It was a long process, taking much fuel. He allowed me to eat supper and breakfast with him and his family, which honor I scarcely deserved. The old man said grace standing up. Then we sat down and he said another. The first was just family prayers. The second was thanksgiving for the meal. The table was so richly and delicately provided that within my heart I paraphrased the twenty-third Psalm, though I did not quote it out aloud: "Thou preparest a table before me in the presence of mine enemies"— (namely, the thunder and lightning, and the inhospitable white man!).

I hope to be rained on again if it brings me communion bread like that I ate with my black host. The conversation was about many things, but began religiously; how *"Ol' Master in the sky gave us everything here to take keer of, and said we mussent waste any of it."* The wife was a mixture of charming diffidence and eagerness in offering her opinion on these points of political economy and theology.

After supper the old gentleman told me a sweet-singing field-bird I described was called the "Rachel-Jane." He had five children grown and away from home and one sleek first voter still under his roof. The old gentleman asked the inevitable question: "Goin' west harvestin'?"

I said "No" again. Then I spread out and explained *The Village Improvement Parade.* This did not interest the family much, but they would never have done with asking me questions about Lincoln. And the fact that I came from Lincoln's home town was plainly my chief distinction in their eyes. The best bed was provided for me, and warm water in which to bathe, and I slept the sleep of the clean and regenerated in snowy linen. Next morning the sun shone, and I walked the muddy roads as cheerfully as though they were the paths of Heaven.

SUNDAY MORNING, JUNE 9, 1912. I am writing in the railroad station at Tipton, Missouri.

A little while back a few people began

to ask me to work for my meals. I believe this is because the "genteel" appearance with which I started has become something else. My derby hat has been used for so many things,—to keep off a Noah's flood of rain, to catch cherries in, to fight bumble-bees, to cover my face while asleep, and keep away the vague terrors of the night,—that it is still a hat, but not quite in the mode. My face is baked by the sun and my hands are fried and stewed. My trousers are creased not in one place, but all over. These things made me look more like a person who, in the words of the conventional world, *"ought to work."*

Having been requested to work once or twice, I immediately made it my custom to offer labor-power as a preliminary to the meal. I generally ask about five people before I find the one who happens to be in a meal-giving mood. This kindly person, about two-thirds of the time, refuses to let me work. I insist and insist, but he says,

THE GOSPEL OF BEAUTY

"Aw, come in and eat anyway." The man
who accepts my offer of work may let me
cut weeds, or hoe corn or potatoes, but he
generally shows me the woodpile and the
axe. Even then every thud of that inevitably dull instrument seems to go through
him. After five minutes he thinks I have
worked an hour, and he comes to the porch
and shouts: "Come in and get your dinner."

Assuming a meal is worth thirty-five
cents, I have never yet worked out the worth
of one, at day-laborer's wages. Very often
I am called into the house three times before
I come. Whether I work or not, the meals
are big and good. Perhaps there is a little
closer attention to *The Gospel of Beauty,*
after three unheeded calls to dinner.

After the kindling is split and the meal
eaten and they lean back in their chairs,
a-weary of their mirth, by one means or another I show them how I am knocking at

the door of the world with a dream in my hand.

Because of the multitudes of tramps pouring west on the freight trains,—tramps I never see because I let freight cars alone,—night accommodations are not so easy to get as they were in my other walks in Pennsylvania and Georgia. I have not yet been forced to sleep under the stars, but each evening has been a scramble. There must be some better solution to this problem of a sleeping-place.

The country hotel, if there is one around, is sometimes willing to take in the man who flatly says he is broke. For instance, the inn-keeper's wife at Clarksburg was tenderly pitiful, yea, she was kind to me after the fashion of the holiest of the angels. There was a protracted meeting going on in the town. That was, perhaps, the reason for her exalted heart. But, whatever the reason, in this one case I was welcomed with such kindness and awe that I dared not lift up my haughty head or distribute my poems, or give tongue to my views, or let her suspect for a moment I was a special IDEA on legs. It was much lovelier to have her think I was utterly forlorn.

This morning when I said good-bye I fumbled my hat, mumbled my words and shuffled my feet, and may the Good St. Francis reward her.

When I asked the way to Tipton the farmer wanted me to walk the railroad. People cannot see "why the Sam Hill" anyone wants to walk the highway when the rails make a bee-line for the destination. This fellow was so anxious for the preservation of my feet he insisted it looked like rain. I finally agreed that, for the sake of avoiding a wetting, I had best hurry to Tipton by the ties. The six miles of railroad between Clarksburg and Tipton should be visited by every botanist in the United States. Skip the rest of this letter unless you are interested in a catalogue of flowers.

THROUGH MISSOURI

First comes the reed with the deep blue blossoms at the top that has bloomed by my path all the way from Springfield, Illinois. Then come enormous wild roses, showing every hue that friend of man ever displayed. Behold an army of white poppies join our march, then healthy legions of waving mustard. Our next recruits are tiny golden-hearted ragged kinsmen of the sunflower. No comrades depart from this triumphal march to Tipton. Once having joined us, they continue in our company. The mass of color grows deeper and more subtle each moment. Behold, regiments of pale lavender larkspur. 'Tis an excellent garden, the finer that it needs no tending. Though the rain has failed to come, I begin to be glad I am hobbling along over the vexatious ties. I forget my resolve to run for President.

Once I determined to be a candidate. I knew I would get the tramp-vote and the actor-vote. My platform was to be that railroad ties should be just close enough for men to walk on them in natural steps, neither mincing the stride nor widely stretching the legs.

Not yet have we reached Tipton. Behold a white flower, worthy of a better name, that the farmers call "sheep's tea." Behold purple larkspur joining the lavender larkspur. Behold that disreputable camp-follower the button-weed, wearing its shabby finery. Now a red delicate grass joins in, and a big purple and pink sort of an aster. Behold a pink and white sheep's tea. And look, there is a dwarf morning glory, the sweetest in the world. Here is a group of black-eyed Susans, marching like suffragettes to get the vote at Tipton. Here is a war-dance of Indian Paint. And here are bluebells.

"Goin' west harvestin'?"

"I have harvested already, ten thousand flowers an hour."

THROUGH MISSOURI

JUNE 10, 1912. 3 p. m. Three miles west of Sedalia, Missouri. In the woods. Near the automobile road to Kansas City.

Now that I have passed Sedalia I am pretty well on toward the Kansas line. Only three more days' journey, and then I shall be in Kansas, State of Romance, State of Expectation. Goodness knows Missouri has plenty of incident, plenty of merit. But it is a cross between Illinois and northern Kentucky, and to beg here is like begging in my own back-yard.

But the heart of Kansas is the heart of the West......... Inclosed find a feather from the wing of a young chicken-hawk. He happened across the road day before yesterday. The farmer stopped the team and killed him with his pitchfork. That farmer seemed to think he had done the Lord a service in ridding the world of a parasite. Yet I had a certain fellow-feeling for the hawk, as I have for anybody who likes chicken.

THE GOSPEL OF BEAUTY

This walk is full of suggestions for poems. Sometimes, in a confidential moment, I tell my hosts I am going to write a chronicle of the whole trip in verse. But I cannot write it now. The traveller at my stage is in a kind of farm-hand condition of mind and blood. He feels himself so much a part of the soil and the sun and the ploughed acres, he eats so hard and sleeps so hard, he has little more patience in trying to write than the husbandman himself.

If that poem is ever written I shall say,—to my fellow-citizens of Springfield, for instance:—"I have gone as your delegate to greet the fields, to claim them for you against a better day. I lay hold on these furrows on behalf of all those cooped up in cities."

I feel that in a certain mystical sense I have made myself part of the hundreds and hundreds of farms that lie between me and machine-made America. I have scarcely seen anything but crops since I left home.

THROUGH MISSOURI

The whole human race is grubbing in the soil, and the soil is responding with tremendous vigor. By walking I get as tired as any and imagine I work too. Sometimes the glory goes. Then I feel my own idleness above all other facts on earth. I want to get to work immediately. But I suppose I am a minstrel or nothing. (There goes a squirrel through the treetops.)

Every time I say "No" to the question "Goin' west harvestin'?" I am a little less brisk about reciting that triad of poems that I find is the best brief exposition of my gospel: (1) *The Proud Farmer*, (2) *The Illinois Village* and (3) *The Building of Springfield*.

If I do harvest it is likely to be just as it was at the Springfield water-works a year ago, when I broke my back in a week trying to wheel bricks.

JUNE 12, 1912. On the banks of a stream west of the town of Warrensburg, Missouri.

THE GOSPEL OF BEAUTY

Perhaps the problem of a night's lodging has been solved. I seem to have found a substitute for the spare bedrooms and white sheets of Georgia and Pennsylvania. It appears that no livery stable will refuse a man a place to sleep. What happened at Otterville and Warrensburg I can make happen from here on, or so I am assured by a farmhand. He told me that every tiniest village from here to western Kansas has at least two livery-stables and there a man may sleep for the asking. He should try to get permission to mount to the hay-mow, for, unless the cot in the office is a mere stretch of canvas, it is likely to be (excuse me) verminiferous. The stable man asks if the mendicant has matches or tobacco. If he has he must give them up. Also he is told not to poke his head far out of the loft window, for, if the insurance man caught him, it would be all up with the insurance. These preliminaries quickly settled, the transient requests a buggy-robe to sleep in, lest he be overwhelmed with the loan of a horse-blanket. The objection to a horse-blanket is that it is a horse-blanket.

And so, if I am to believe my friend with the red neck, my good times at Warrensburg and Otterville are likely to continue.

Strange as it may seem, sleeping in a hay-loft is Romance itself. The alfalfa is soft and fragrant and clean, the wind blows through the big loft door, the stars shine through the cottonwoods. If I wake in the night I hear the stable-boys bringing in the teams of men who have driven a long way and back again to get something;—to get drunk, or steal the kisses of somebody's wife or put over a political deal or get a chance to preach a sermon;—and I get scraps of detail from the stable-boys after the main actors of the drama have gone. It sounds as though all the remarks were being made in the loft instead of on the ground floor. The horses stamp and stamp and the grinding sound of their teeth is so close to me I

cannot believe at first that the mangers and
feed-boxes are way down below.

It is morning before I know it and the
gorged birds are singing "shivaree, shivaree, Rachel Jane, Rachel Jane" in the mulberry trees, just outside the loft window.
After a short walk I negotiate for breakfast, then walk on through Paradise and at
the proper time negotiate for dinner, walk
on through Paradise again and at six negotiate for the paradisical haymow, without
looking for supper, and again more sleepy
than hungry. The difference between this
system and the old one is that about half
past four I used to begin to worry about
supper and night accommodations, and generally worried till seven. Now life is one
long sweet stroll, and I watch the sunset
from my bed in the alfalfa with the delights
of the whole day renewed in my heart.

Passing through the village of Sedalia I
inquired the way out of town to the main
road west. My informant was a man named

THROUGH MISSOURI

McSweeny, drunk enough to be awfully friendly. He asked all sorts of questions. He induced me to step two blocks out of my main course down a side-street to his "Restaurant." He said he was not going to let me leave town without a square meal. It was a strange eating-place, full of ditch-diggers, teamsters, red-necked politicians and slender intellectual politicians. In the background was a scattering of the furtive daughters of pleasure, some white, some black. The whole institution was but an annex to the bar room in front. Mr. Mc-Sweeny looked over my book while I ate. After the meal he gathered a group of the politicians and commanded me to recite. I gave them my rhyme in memory of Altgeld and my rhyme in denunciation of Lorimer, and my rhyme denouncing all who coöper-ated in the white slave trade, including sell-ers of drink. Mr. McSweeny said I was the goods, and offered to pass the hat, but I would not permit. A handsome black jezebel sat as near us as she dared and listened quite seriously. I am sure she would have put something in that hat if it had gone round.

"I suppose," said Mr. McSweeny, as he stood at his door to bow adieu, "you will harvest when you get a little further west?"

That afternoon I walked miles and miles through rough country, and put up with a friendly farmer named John Humphrey. He had children like little golden doves, and a most hard-working wife. The man had harvested and travelled eight years in the west before he had settled down. He told me all about it. Until late that night he told me endless fascinating stories upon the theme of that free man's land ahead of me. If he had not had those rosy babies to anchor him, he would have picked up and gone along, and argued down my rule to travel alone.

Because he had been a man of the road there was a peculiar feeling of understanding in the air. They were people of much natural refinement. I was the more grateful for their bread when I considered that when I came upon them at sunset they were working together in the field. There was not a hand to help. How could they be so happy and seem so blest? Their day was nearer sixteen than eight hours long. I felt deathly ashamed to eat their bread. I told them so, with emphasis. But the mother said, "We always takes in them that asks, and nobody never done us no harm yet."

That night was a turning point with me. In reply to a certain question I said: *"Yes. I am going west harvesting."*

I asked the veteran traveller to tell me the best place to harvest. He was sitting on the floor pulling the children's toes, and having a grand time. He drew himself up into a sort of oracular knot, with his chin on his knees, and gesticulated with his pipe.

"Go straight west," he said, "to Great Bend, Barton County, Kansas, the banner

THE GOSPEL OF BEAUTY

wheat county of the United States. Arrive
about July fifth. Walk to the public square.
Walk two miles north. Look around. You
will see nothing but wheat fields, and farmers standing on the edge of the road crying
into big red handkerchiefs. Ask the first
man for work. He will stop crying and
give it to you. Wages will be two dollars
and a half a day, and keep. You will have
all you want to eat and a clean blanket in
the hay."

I have resolved to harvest at Great Bend.

HEART OF GOD

A PRAYER IN THE JUNGLES OF HEAVEN

O great Heart of God,
Once vague and lost to me,
Why do I throb with your throb to-night,
In this land, Eternity?
O little Heart of God,
Sweet intruding stranger,
You are laughing in my human breast,
A Christ-child in a manger.
Heart, dear Heart of God,

THROUGH MISSOURI

Beside you now I kneel,
Strong Heart of Faith. O Heart not mine,
Where God has set His seal.
Wild thundering Heart of God
Out of my doubt I come,
And my foolish feet with prophets' feet,
March with the prophets' drum.

III

Walking into Kansas

IT has been raining quite a little. The roads are so muddy I have to walk the ties. Keeping company with the railroad is almost a habit. While this shower passes I write in the station at Stillwell, Kansas.

JUNE 14, 1912. I have crossed the mystic border. I have left Earth. I have entered Wonderland. Though I am still east of the geographical centre of the United States, in every spiritual sense I am in the West. This morning I passed the stone mile-post that marks the beginning of Kansas.

I went over the border and encountered —what do you think? Wild strawberries! Lo, where the farmer had cut the weeds between the road and the fence, the gentle fruits revealed themselves, growing in the shadow down between the still-standing weeds. They shine out in a red line that stretches on and on, and a man has to resolve to stop eating several times. Just as he thinks he has conquered desire the line gets dazzlingly red again.

The berries grow at the end of a slender stalk, clustered six in a bunch. One gathers them by the stems, in bouquets, as it were, and eats off the fruit like taffy off a stick.

I was gathering buckets of cherries for a farmer's wife yesterday. This morning after the strawberries had mitigated I encountered a bush of raspberries, and then hedges on hedges of mulberries both white and red. The white mulberries are the sweetest. If this is the wild West, give me more. There are many varieties of trees, and they are thick as in the East. The people seem to grow more cordial. I was eating mulberries outside the yard of a villager. He asked me in where the eating was better. And then he told me the town scandal, while I had my dessert.

A day or so ago I hoed corn all morning for my dinner. This I did cheerfully, considering I had been given a good breakfast at that farm for nothing. I feel that two good meals are worth about a morning's work anyway. And then I had company. The elderly owner of the place hoed along with me. He saved the country, by preaching to me the old fashioned high tariff gospel, and I saved it by preaching to him the new fashioned Gospel of Beauty. Meanwhile the corn was hoed. Then we went in and ate the grandest of dinners. That house was notable for having on its walls really artistic pictures, not merely respectable pictures, nor yet seed-catalogue advertisements.

That night, in passing through a village, I glimpsed a man washing his dishes in the rear of a blacksmith shop. I said to myself: "Ah ha! Somebody keeping bach."

I knew I was welcome. There is no fear of the stranger in such a place, for there are no ladies to reassure or propitiate. Permission to sleep on the floor was granted as soon as asked. I spread out *The Kansas City Star,* which is a clean sheet, put my verses under my head for a pillow and was content. Next morning the sun was in my eyes. There was the odor of good fried bacon in the air.

"Git up and eat a snack, pardner," said my friend the blacksmith. And while I ate he told me the story of his life.

I had an amusing experience at the town of Belton. I had given an entertainment at the hotel on the promise of a night's lodging. I slept late. Over my transom came the breakfast-table talk. "That was a hot entertainment that young bum gave us last night," said one man. "He ought to get to work, the dirty lazy loafer," said another.

THE GOSPEL OF BEAUTY

The schoolmaster spoke up in an effort not to condescend to his audience: "He is evidently a fraud. I talked to him a long time after the entertainment. The pieces he recited were certainly not his own. I have read some of them somewhere. It is too easy a way to get along, especially when the man is as able to work as this one. Of course in the old days literary men used to be obliged to do such things. But it isn't at all necessary in the Twentieth Century. Real poets are highly paid." Another spoke up: "I don't mind a fake, but he is a rotten reciter, anyhow. If he had said one more I would have just walked right out. You noticed ol' Mis' Smith went home after that piece about the worms." Then came the landlord's voice: "After the show was over I came pretty near not letting him have his room. All I've got to say is he don't get any breakfast."

I dressed, opened the doorway serenely, and strolled past the table, smiling with all the ease of a minister at his own church-social. In my most ornate manner I thanked the landlord and landlady for their extreme kindness. I assumed that not one of the gentle-folk had intended to have me hear their analysis. 'Twas a grand exit. Yet, in plain language, these people "got my goat." I have struggled with myself all morning, almost on the point of ordering a marked copy of a magazine sent to that smart schoolmaster. *"Evidently a fraud!"* Indeed!

"Goin' wes' harvesin'?"

"Yes, yes. I think I will harvest when I get to Great Bend."

JUNE 18, 1912. Approaching Emporia. I am sitting in the hot sun by the Santa Fé tracks, after two days of walking those tracks in the rain. I am near a queer little Mexican house built of old railroad ties.

I had had two sticks of candy begged from a grocer for breakfast. I was keeping warm by walking fast. Because of the muddy roads and the sheets of rain coming down it was impossible to leave the tracks. It was almost impossible to make speed since the ballast underfoot was almost all of it big rattling broken stone. I had walked that Santa Fé railroad a day and a half in the drizzle and downpour. It was a little past noon, and my scanty inner fuel was almost used up. I dared not stop a minute now, lest I catch cold. There was no station in sight ahead. When the mists lifted I saw that the tracks went on and on, straight west to the crack of doom, not even a water-tank in sight. The mists came down, then lifted once more, and, as though I were Childe Roland, I suddenly saw a shack to the right, in dimensions about seven feet each way. It was mostly stove-pipe, and that pipe was pouring out enough smoke to make three of Aladdin's Jinns. I presume some one heard me whistling. The little door opened. Two heads popped out, "Come in, you slab-sided hobo," they yelled affectionately. "Come in and get dry." And so my heart was made suddenly light after a day and a half of hard whistling.

At the inside end of that busy smokestack was a roaring redhot stove about as big as a hat. It had just room enough on top for three steaming coffee cans at a time. There were four white men with their chins on their knees completely occupying the floor of one side of the mansion, and four Mexicans filled the other. Every man was hunched up to take as little room as possible. It appeared that my only chance was to move the tins and sit on the stove. But one Mexican sort of sat on another Mexican and the new white man was accommodated. These fellows were a double-section gang, for the track is double all along here.

I dried out pretty quick. The men began to pass up the coffee off the stove. It strangled and blistered me, it was so hot. The men were almost to the bottom of the food sections of their buckets and were be-

THE GOSPEL OF BEAUTY

ginning to throw perfectly good sandwiches and extra pieces of pie through the door. I said that if any man had anything to throw away would he just wait till I stepped outside so I could catch it. They handed me all I could ever imagine a man eating. It rained and rained and rained, and I ate till I could eat no more. One man gave me for dessert the last half of his cup of stewed raisins along with his own spoon. Good raisins they were, too. A Mexican urged upon me some brown paper and cigarette tobacco. I was sorry I did not smoke. The men passed up more and more hot coffee.

That coffee made me into a sort of thermos bottle. On the strength of it I walked all afternoon through sheets and cataracts. When dark came I slept in wet clothes in a damp blanket in the hay of a windy livery-stable without catching cold.

Now it is morning. The sky is reasonably clear, the weather is reasonably warm, but I am no longer a thermos bottle, no, no. I am sitting on the hottest rock I can find, letting the sun go through my bones. The coffee in me has turned at last to ice and snow. Emporia, the Athens of America, is just ahead. Oh, for a hot bath and a clean shirt!

A mad dog tried to bite me yesterday morning, when I made a feeble attempt to leave the track. When I was once back on the ties, he seemed afraid and would not come closer. His bark was the ghastliest thing I ever heard. As for his bite, he did not get quite through my shoe-heel.

EMPORIA, KANSAS, JUNE 19, 1912. On inquiring at the Emporia General Delivery for mail, I found your letter telling me to call upon your friend Professor Kerr. He took my sudden appearance most kindly, and pardoned my battered attire and the mud to the knees. After a day in his house I am ready to go on, dry and feasted and warm and clean. The professor's help seemed to come in just in time. I was a most weary creature.

Thinking it over this morning, the bath-tub appears to be the first outstanding advantage the cultured man has over the half-civilized. Quite often the folk with swept houses and decent cooking who have given my poems discriminating attention, who have given me good things to eat, forget, even when they entertain him overnight, that the stranger would like to soak himself thoroughly. Many of the working people seem to keep fairly clean with the washpan as their principal ally. But the tub is indispensable to the mendicant in the end, unless he is walking through a land of crystal waterfalls, like North Georgia.

I am an artificial creature at last, dependent, after all, upon modern plumbing. 'Tis, perhaps, not a dignified theme, but I retired to the professor's bathroom and washed off the entire State of Missouri and the eastern counties of Kansas, and did a deal of laundry work on the sly. This last was not openly confessed to the professor, but he might have guessed, I was so cold on the front porch that night.

I shall not soon lose the memory of this the first day of emergence from the strait paths of St. Francis, this first meeting, since I left Springfield, with a person on whom I had a conventional social claim. I had forgotten what the delicacy of a cultured welcome would be like. The professor's table was a marvel to me. I was astonished to discover there were such fine distinctions in food and linen. And for all my troubadour profession, I had almost forgotten there were such distinctions in books. I have hardly seen one magazine since I left you. The world where I have been moving reads nothing but newspapers. It is confusing to bob from one world to the other, to zig-zag across the social dead-line. I sat in the professor's library a very mixed-up person, feeling I could hardly stay a minute, yet too heavy-footed to stir an inch, and immensely grateful and relaxed.

Sooner or later I am going to step up into the rarefied civilized air once too often and stay there in spite of myself. I shall get a little too fond of the china and old silver, and forget the fields. Books and teacups and high-brow conversations are awfully insinuating things, if you give them time to be. One gets along somehow, and pleasure alternates with pain, and the sum is the joy of life, while one is below. But to quit is like coming up to earth after deep-sea diving in a heavy suit. One scarcely realizes he has been under heavier-than-air pressure, and has been fighting off great forces, till he has taken off his diving helmet, as it were. And yet there is a baffling sense of futility in the restful upper air. I remember it once, long ago, in emerging in Warren, Ohio, and once in emerging in Macon, Georgia:—the feeling that the upper world is all tissue paper,

WALKING INTO KANSAS

that the only choice a real man can make is to stay below with the great forces of life forever, even though he be a tramp—the feeling that, to be a little civilized, we sacrifice enormous powers and joys. For all I was so tired and so very grateful to the professor, I felt like a bull in a china shop. I should have been out in the fields, eating grass.

THE KALLYOPE YELL

[*Loudly and rapidly with a leader, College yell fashion*]

I

Proud men
Eternally
Go about,
Slander me,
Call me the "Calliope."
Sizz . . . . .
Fizz . . . . .

II

I am the Gutter Dream,
Tune-maker, born of steam,
Tooting joy, tooting hope.
I am the Kallyope,
Car called the Kallyope.
Willy willy willy wah HOO!
See the flags: snow-white tent,
See the bear and elephant,
See the monkey jump the rope,
Listen to the Kallyope, Kallyope, Kallyope!
Soul of the rhinoceros
And the hippopotamus
(Listen to the lion roar!)
Jaguar, cockatoot,
Loons, owls,
Hoot, Hoot.
Listen to the lion roar,
Listen to the lion roar,
Listen to the lion R-O-A-R!
Hear the leopard cry for gore,
Willy willy willy wah HOO!

WALKING INTO KANSAS

Hail the bloody Indian band,
Hail, all hail the popcorn stand,
Hail to Barnum's picture there,
People's idol everywhere,
Whoop, whoop, whoop, WHOOP!
Music of the mob am I,
Circus day's tremendous cry:—
I am the Kallyope, Kallyope, Kallyope!
Hoot toot, hoot toot, hoot toot, hoot toot,
Willy willy willy wah HOO!
Sizz, fizz . . . . .

III

Born of mobs, born of steam,
Listen to my golden dream,
Listen to my golden dream,
Listen to my G-O-L-D-E-N D-R-E-A-M!
Whoop whoop whoop whoop WHOOP!
I will blow the proud folk low,
Humanize the dour and slow,
I will shake the proud folk down,
(Listen to the lion roar!)
Popcorn crowds shall rule the town—

THE GOSPEL OF BEAUTY

Willy willy willy wah ноо!
Steam shall work melodiously,
Brotherhood increase.
You'll see the world and all it holds
For fifty cents apiece.
Willy willy willy wah ноо!
Every day a circus day.

What?

Well, *almost* every day.
Nevermore the sweater's den,
Nevermore the prison pen.
Gone the war on land and sea
That aforetime troubled men.
Nations all in amity,
Happy in their plumes arrayed
In the long bright street parade.
Bands a-playing every day.

What?

Well, *almost* every day.
I am the Kallyope, Kallyope, Kallyope!

WALKING INTO KANSAS

Willy willy willy wah HOO!
Hoot, toot, hoot, toot,
Whoop whoop whoop whoop,
Willy willy willy wah HOO!
Sizz, fizz . . . . .

IV

Every soul
Resident
In the earth's one circus tent!
Every man a trapeze king
Then a pleased spectator there.
On the benches!   In the ring!
While the neighbors gawk and stare
And the cheering rolls along.
Almost every day a race
When the merry starting gong
Rings, each chariot on the line,
Every driver fit and fine
With the steel-spring Roman grace.
Almost every day a dream,
Almost every day a dream.
Every girl,

THE GOSPEL OF BEAUTY

Maid or wife,
Wild with music,
Eyes a-gleam
With that marvel called desire:
Actress, princess, fit for life,
Armed with honor like a knife,
Jumping thro' the hoops of fire.
(Listen to the lion roar!)
Making all the children shout
Clowns shall tumble all about,
Painted high and full of song
While the cheering rolls along,
Tho' they scream,
Tho' they rage,
Every beast
In his cage,
Every beast
In his den
That aforetime troubled men.

WALKING INTO KANSAS

V

I am the Kallyope, Kallyope, Kallyope,
Tooting hope, tooting hope, tooting hope,
    tooting hope;
Shaking window-pane and door
With a crashing cosmic tune,
With the war-cry of the spheres,
Rhythm of the roar of noon,
Rhythm of Niagara's roar,
Voicing planet, star and moon,
SHRIEKING of the better years.
Prophet-singers will arise,
Prophets coming after me,
Sing my song in softer guise
With more delicate surprise;
I am but the pioneer
Voice of the Democracy;
I am the gutter dream,
I am the golden dream,
Singing science, singing steam.
I will blow the proud folk down,

THE GOSPEL OF BEAUTY

(Listen to the lion roar!)
I am the Kallyope, Kallyope, Kallyope,
Tooting hope, tooting hope, tooting hope,
   tooting hope,
Willy willy willy wah HOO!
Hoot, toot, hoot toot, hoot toot, hoot toot,
Whoop whoop, whoop whoop,
Whoop whoop, whoop whoop,
Willy willy willy wah HOO!
Sizz . . . . .
Fizz . . . . .

SUNDAY MORNING, JUNE 23, 1912. I am writing on the top of a pile of creosote-soaked ties between the Santa Fé tracks and the trail that runs parallel to the tracks. Florence, Kansas, is somewhere ahead.

In the East the railroads and machinery choke the land to death and it was there I made my rule against them. But the farther West I go the more the very life of the country seems to depend upon them. I suppose, though, that some day, even out West here, the rule against the railroad will be a good rule.

Meanwhile let me say that my Ruskinian prejudices are temporarily overcome by the picturesqueness and efficiency of the Santa Fé. It is double-tracked, and every four miles is kept in order by a hand-car crew that is spinning back and forth all the time. The air seems to be full of hand-cars.

Walking in a hurry to make a certain place by nightfall I have become acquainted with these section hands, and, most delightful to relate, have ridden in their iron conveyances, putting my own back into the work. Half or three-fourths of the employees are Mexicans who are as ornamental in the actual landscape as they are in a Remington drawing. These Mexicans are tractable serfs of the Santa Fé. If there were enough miles of railroad in Mexico to keep all the inhabitants busy on section, perhaps the internal difficulties could be ended. These peons live peacefully next to the tracks in houses built by the company from old ties. The ties are placed on end, side by side, with plaster in the cracks, on a tiny oblong two-room plan. There is a little roofed court between the rooms. A farmer told me that the company tried Greek serfs for a while, but they made trouble for out-siders and murdered each other.

The road is busy as busy can be. Almost any time one can see enormous freight-trains rolling by or mile-a-minute passenger trains. Gates are provided for each farmer's right of way. I was told by an exceptional Mexican with powers of speech that the efficient dragging of the wagon-roads, especially the "New Santa Fé Trail" that follows the railroad, is owing to the missionary work of King, the split-log drag man, who was employed to go up and down this land agitating his hobby.

When the weather is good, touring auto-mobiles whiz past. They have pennants showing they are from Kansas City, Emporia, New York or Chicago. They have camping canvas and bedding on the back seats of the car, or strapped in the rear. They are on camping tours to Colorado Springs and the like pleasure places. Some few avow they are going to the coast. About five o'clock in the evening some man making a local trip is apt to come along alone. He it is that wants the other side of the machine weighed down. He it is that will offer me a ride and spin me along from five to twenty-five miles before supper. This delightful use that may be made of an automobile in rounding out a day's walk has had something to do with mending my prejudice against it, despite the grand airs of the tourists that whirl by at midday. I still maintain that the auto is a carnal institution, to be shunned by the truly spiritual, but there are times when I, for one, get tired of being spiritual.

Much of the country east of Emporia is hilly and well-wooded and hedged like Missouri. But now I am getting into the range region. Yesterday, after several miles of treeless land that had never known the plough, I said to myself: "Now I am really West." And my impression was reinforced when I reached a grand baronial establishment called "Clover Hill Ranch." It was flanked by the houses of the retainers. In the foreground and a little to the side was the great stone barn for the mules and horses. Back on the little hill, properly introduced by ceremonious trees, was the ranch house itself. And before it was my lord on his ranching charger. The aforesaid lord created quite an atmosphere of lordliness as he refused work in the alfalfa harvest to a battered stranger who bowed too low and begged too hard, perhaps. On the porch was my lady, feeding bread and honey to the beautiful young prince of the place.

I have not yet reached the wheat belt. Since the alfalfa harvest is on here, I shall try for that a bit.

WALKING INTO KANSAS

SUNDAY AFTERNOON, JUNE 30, 1912. In the spare room of a Mennonite farmer, who lives just inside the wheat belt.

This is going to be a long Sunday afternoon; so make up your minds for a long letter. I did not get work in the alfalfa. Yet there is news. I have been staying a week with this Mennonite family shocking wheat for them, though I am not anywhere near Great Bend.

Before I tell you of the harvest, I must tell you of these Mennonites. They are a dear people. I have heard from their reverent lips the name of their founder, Menno Simonis, who was born about the time of Columbus and Luther and other such worthies. They are as opposed to carnal literature as I am to tailor-made clothes, and I hold they are perfectly correct in allowing no fashion magazines in the house. Such modern books as they read deal with practical local philanthropies and great international mission movements, and their interdenominational feelings for all Christendom are strong. Yet they hold to their ancient verities, and antiquity broods over their meditations.

For instance I found in their bookcase an endless dialogue epic called *The Wandering Soul,* in which this soul, seeking mainly for information, engages in stilted conversation with Adam, Noah, and Simon Cleophas. Thereby the Wandering Soul is informed as to the orthodox history and chronology of the world from the Creation to the destruction of Jerusalem. The wood-cuts are devotional. They are worth walking to Kansas to see. The book had its third translation into Pennsylvania English in 1840, but several American editions had existed in German before that, and several German editions in Germany. It was originally written in the Dutch language and was popular among the Mennonites there. But it looks as if it was printed by Adam to last forever and scare bad boys.

WALKING INTO KANSAS

Let us go to meeting. All the women are on their own side of the aisle. All of them have a fairly uniform Quakerish sort of dress of no prescribed color. In front are the most pious, who wear a black scoop-bonnet. Some have taken this off, and show the inevitable "prayer-covering" underneath. It is the plainest kind of a lace-cap, awfully coquettish on a pretty head. It is intended to mortify the flesh, and I suppose it *is* unbecoming to *some* women.

All the scoop-bonnets are not black. Toward the middle of the church, behold a cream-satin, a soft gray, a dull moon-gold. One young woman, moved, I fear, by the devil, turns and looks across the aisle at us. An exceedingly demure bow is tied all too sweetly under the chin, in a decorous butterfly style. Fie! fie! Is this mortifying the flesh? And I note with pain that the black bonnets grow fewer and fewer toward the rear of the meeting house.

Here come the children, with bobbing

headgear of every color of the rainbow, yet the same scoop-pattern still. They have been taking little walks and runs between Sunday-school and church, and are all flushed and panting. But I would no more criticise the color of their headgear than the color in their faces. Some of them squeeze in among the black rows in front and make piety reasonable. But we noted by the door as they entered something that both the church and the world must abhor. Seated as near to the men's side as they can get, with a mixture of shame and defiance in their faces, are certain daughters of the Mennonites who insist on dressing after the fashions that come from Paris and Kansas City and Emporia. By the time the rumors of what is proper in millinery have reached this place they are a disconcerting mixture of cherries, feathers and ferns. And somehow there are too many mussy ribbons on the dresses.

We can only guess how these rebels must suffer under the concentrated silent prayers of the godly. Poor honest souls! they take to this world's vain baggage and overdo it. Why do they not make up their minds to serve the devil sideways, like that sly puss with the butterfly bow?

On the men's side of the house the division on dress is more acute. The Holiness movement, the doctrine of the Second Blessing that has stirred many rural Methodist groups, has attacked the Mennonites also. Those who dispute for this new ism of sanctification leave off their neckties as a sign. Those that retain their neckties, satisfied with what Menno Simonis taught, have a hard time remaining in a state of complete calm. The temptation to argue the matter is almost more than flesh can bear.

But, so far as I could discover, there was no silent prayer over the worst lapse of these people. What remains of my Franciscan soul was hurt to discover that the buggy-shed of the meeting-house was full of automobiles. And to meet a Mennonite on the road without a necktie, his wife in the blackest of bonnets, honking along in one of those glittering brazen machines, almost shakes my confidence in the Old Jerusalem Gospel.

Yet let me not indulge in disrespect. Every spiritual warfare must abound in its little ironies. They are keeping their rule against finery as well as I am keeping mine against the railroad. And they have their own way of not being corrupted by money. Their ministry is unsalaried. Their preachers are sometimes helpers on the farms, sometimes taken care of outright, the same as I am.

As will later appear, despite some inconsistencies, the Mennonites have a piety as literal as any to be found on the earth. Since they are German there is no lack of thought in their system. I attended one of their quarterly conferences and I have never heard better discourses on the distinctions between the four gospels. The men who spoke were scholars.

WALKING INTO KANSAS

The Mennonites make it a principle to ignore politics, and are non-resistants in war. I have read in the life of one of their heroes what a terrible time his people had in the Shenandoah valley in the days of Sheridan. . . . Three solemn tracts are here on my dresser. The first is against church organs, embodying a plea for simplicity and the spending of such money on local benevolences and world-wide missions. The tract aptly compares the church-organ to the Thibetan prayer-wheel, and later to praying by phonograph. A song is a prayer to them, and they sing hymns and nothing but hymns all week long.

The next tract is on non-conformity to this world, and insists our appearance should indicate our profession, and that fashions drive the poor away from the church. It condemns jewels and plaiting of the hair, etc., and says that such things stir up a wicked and worldly lust in the eyes of youth. This tract goes so far as to put worldly pictures under the ban. Then comes another, headed Bible Teaching on Dress. It goes on to show that every true Christian, especially that vain bird, the female, should wear something like the Mennonite uniform to indicate the line of separation from "the World." I have a good deal of sympathy for all this, for indeed is it not briefly comprehended in my own rule: "Carry no baggage"?

These people celebrate communion every half year, and at the same time they practise the ritual of washing the feet. Since Isadora Duncan has rediscovered the human foot æsthetically, who dares object to it in ritual? It is all a question of what we are trained to expect. Certainly these people are respecters of the human foot and not ashamed to show it. Next to the way their women have of making a dash to find their gauzy prayer-covering, which they put on for grace at table and Bible-lesson before breakfast, their most striking habit is the way both men and women go about in very clean bare feet after supper. Next to this let me note their resolve to have no profane hour whatsoever. When not actually at work they sit and sing hymns, each Christian on his own hook as he has leisure.

My first evening among these dear strangers I was sitting alone by the front door, looking out on the wheat. I was thrilled to see the fairest member of the household enter, not without grace and dignity. Her prayer covering was on her head, her white feet were shining like those of Nicolette and her white hymn-book was in her hand. She ignored me entirely. She was rapt in trance. She sat by the window and sang through the book, looking straight at a rose in the wall-paper.

I lingered there, reading *The Wandering Soul* just as oblivious of her presence as she was of mine. Oh, no; there was no art in the selection of her songs! I remember one which was to this effect:

THE GOSPEL OF BEAUTY

"Don't let it be said:
'Too late, too late
To enter that Golden Gate.'
Be ready, for soon
The time will come
To enter that Golden Gate."

On the whole she had as much right to plunk down and sing hymns out of season as I have to burst in and quote poetry to peaceful and unprotected households.

I would like to insert a discourse here on the pleasure and the naturalness and the humanness of testifying to one's gospel whatever that gospel may be, barefooted or golden-slippered or iron-shod. The best we may win in return may be but a kindly smile. We may never make one convert. Still the duty of testifying remains, and is enjoined by the invisible powers and makes for the health of the soul. This Mennonite was a priestess of her view of the truth and comes of endless generations of such snow-footed apostles. I presume the sect ceased to enlarge when the Quakers ceased to thrive, but I make my guess that it does not crumble as fast as the Quakers, having more German stolidity.

Let me again go forward, testifying to my particular lonely gospel in the face of such pleasant smiles and incredulous questions as may come. I wish I could start a sturdy sect like old Menno Simonis did. They should dress as these have done, and be as stubborn and rigid in their discipline. They should farm as these have done, but on reaching the point where the Mennonite buys the automobile, that money and energy should go into the making of cross-roads palaces for the people, golden as the harvest field, and disciplined well-parked villages, good as a psalm, and cities fair as a Mennonite lady in her prayer-covering, delicate and noble as Athens the unforgotten, the divine.

The Mennonite doctrine of non-participation in war or politics leads them to confine their periodic literature to religious journals exclusively, plus *The Drover's Journal* to keep them up to date on the prices of farm-products. There is only one Mennonite political event, the coming of Christ to judge the earth. Of that no man knoweth the day or the hour. We had best be prepared and not play politics or baseball or anything. Just keep unspotted and harvest the wheat.

"Goin' wes' harvesin'?"

I have harvested, thank you. Four days and a half I have shocked wheat in these prayer-consecrated fields that I see even now from my window. And I have good hard dollars in my pocket, which same dollars are against my rules.

I will tell you of the harvest in the next letter.

WALKING INTO KANSAS

ON THE ROAD TO NOWHERE

On the road to nowhere
What wild oats did you sow
When you left your father's house
With your cheeks aglow?
Eyes so strained and eager
To see what you might see?
Were you thief or were you fool
Or most nobly free?
Were the tramp-days knightly,
True sowing of wild seed?
Did you dare to make the songs
Vanquished workmen need?
Did you waste much money
To deck a leper's feast?
Love the truth, defy the crowd,
Scandalize the priest?
On the road to nowhere
What wild oats did you sow?
Stupids find the nowhere-road
Dusty, grim and slow.
Ere their sowing's ended
They turn them on their track:
Look at the caitiff craven wights
Repentant, hurrying back!

THE GOSPEL OF BEAUTY

Grown ashamed of nowhere,
Of rags endured for years,
Lust for velvet in their hearts,
Pierced with Mammon's spears.
All but a few fanatics
Give up their darling goal,
Seek to be as others are,
Stultify the soul.
Reapings now confront them,
Glut them, or destroy,
Curious seeds, grain or weeds,
Sown with awful joy.
Hurried is their harvest,
They make soft peace with men.
Pilgrims pass. They care not,
Will not tramp again.
O nowhere, golden nowhere!
Sages and fools go on
To your chaotic ocean,
To your tremendous dawn.
Far in your fair dream-haven,
Is nothing or is all . . .
They press on, singing, sowing
Wild deeds without recall!

IV

In Kansas: The First Harvest

MONDAY AFTERNOON, JULY 1, 1912. A little west of Newton, Kansas. In the public library of a village whose name I forget.

Here is the story of how I came to harvest. I was by chance taking a short respite from the sunshine, last Monday noon, on the porch of the Mennonite farmer. I had had dinner further back. But the good folk asked me to come in and have dessert anyway. It transpired that one of the two harvest hands was taking his farewell meal. He was obliged to fill a contract to work further West, a contract made last year. I timidly suggested I might take his place. To my astonishment I was engaged at once. This fellow was working for two dollars a day, but I agreed to $1.75, seeing my predecessor was a skilled man and twice as big as I was. My wages, as I discovered, included three rich meals, and a pretty spare room to sleep in, and a good big bucket to bathe in nightly.

I anticipate history at this point by telling how at the end of the week my wages looked as strange to me as a bunch of unexpected ducklets to a hen. They were as curious to contemplate as a group of mischievous nieces who have come to spend the day with their embarrassed, fluttering maiden aunt.

I took my wages to Newton, and spent all on the vanities of this life. First the grandest kind of a sombrero, so I shall not be sun-struck in the next harvest-field, which I narrowly escaped in this. Next, the most indestructible of corduroys. Then I had my shoes re-soled and bought a necktie that was like the oriflamme of Navarre, and attended to several other points of vanity. I started out again, dead broke and happy.

THE FIRST HARVEST

If I work hereafter I can send most all my wages home, for I am now in real travelling costume.

But why linger over the question of wages till I show I earned those wages?

Let me tell you of a typical wheat-harvesting day. The field is two miles from the house. We make preparations for a twelve-hour siege. Halters and a barrel of water and a heap of alfalfa for the mules, binder-twine and oil for the reaper and water-jugs for us are loaded into the spring wagon. Two mules are hitched in front, two are led behind. The new reaper was left in the field yesterday. We make haste. We must be at work by the time the dew dries. The four mules are soon hitched to the reaper and proudly driven into the wheat by the son of the old Mennonite. This young fellow carries himself with proper dignity as heir of the farm. He is a credit to the father. He will not curse the mules, though those animals forget their religion sometimes, and act after the manner of their kind. The worst he will do will be to call one of them an old cow. I suppose when he is vexed with a cow he calls it an old mule. My other companion is a boy of nineteen from a Mennonite community in Pennsylvania. He sets me a pace. Together we build the sheaves into shocks, of eight or ten sheaves each, put so they will not be shaken by an ordinary Kansas wind. The wind has been blowing nearly all the time at a rate which in Illinois would mean a thunderstorm in five minutes, and sometimes the clouds loom in the thunderstorm way, yet there is not a drop of rain, and the clouds are soon gone.

In the course of the week the boy and I have wrestled with heavy ripe sheaves, heavier green sheaves, sheaves full of Russian thistles and sheaves with the string off. The boy, as he sings *The day-star hath risen,* twists a curious rope of straw and reties the loose bundles with one turn of the hand.

THE FIRST HARVEST

I try, but cannot make the knot. Once all sheaves were so bound.

Much of the wheat must be cut heavy and green because there is a liability to sudden storms or hail that will bury it in mud, or soften the ground and make it impossible to drag the reaper, or hot winds that suddenly ripen the loose grain and shake it into the earth. So it is an important matter to get the wheat out when it is anywhere near ready. I found that two of the girls were expecting to take the place of the departing hand, if I had not arrived.

The Mennonite boy picked up two sheaves to my one at the beginning of the week. To-day I learn to handle two at a time and he immediately handles three at a time. He builds the heart of the sheaf. Then we add the outside together. He is always marching ahead and causing me to feel ashamed.

The Kansas grasshopper makes himself friendly. He bites pieces out of the back of my shirt the shape and size of the ace of spades. Then he walks into the door he has made and loses himself. Then he has to be helped out, in one way or another.

The old farmer, too stiff for work, comes out on his dancing pony and rides behind the new reaper. This reaper was bought only two days ago and he beams with pride upon it. It seems that he and his son almost swore, trying to tinker the old one. The farmer looks with even more pride upon the field, still a little green, but mostly golden. He dismounts and tests the grain, threshing it out in his hand, figuring the average amount in several typical heads. He stands off, and is guilty of an æsthetic thrill. He says of the sea of gold: "I wish I could have a photograph of that." (O eloquent word, for a Mennonite!) Then he plays at building half a dozen shocks, then goes home till late in the afternoon. We three are again masters of the field.

We are in a level part of Kansas, not a rolling range as I found it further east.

THE FIRST HARVEST

The field is a floor. Hedges gradually faded from the landscape in counties several days' journey back, leaving nothing but unbroken billows to the horizon. But the hedges have been resumed in this region. Each time round the enormous field we stop at a break in the line of those untrimmed old thorn-trees. Here we rest a moment and drink from the water-jug. To keep from getting sunstruck I profanely waste the water, pouring it on my head, and down my neck to my feet. I came to this farm wearing a derby, and have had to borrow a slouch with a not-much-wider rim from the farmer. It was all the extra headgear available in this thrifty region. Because of that not-much-wider rim my face is sunburned all over every day. I have not yet received my wages to purchase my sombrero.

As we go round the field, the Mennonite boy talks religion, or is silent. I have caught the spirit of the farm, and sing all the hymn-tunes I can remember. Sometimes the wind turns hot. Perspiration cannot keep up with evaporation. Our skins are dry as the dryest stubble. Then we stand and wait for a little streak of cool wind. It is pretty sure to come in a minute. "That's a nice air," says the boy, and gets to work. Once it was so hot all three of us stopped five minutes by the hedge. Then it was I told them the story of the hens I met just west of Emporia.

I had met ten hens walking single-file into the town of Emporia. I was astonished to meet educated hens. Each one was swearing. I would not venture, I added, to repeat what they said.

Not a word from the Mennonites.

I continued in my artless way, showing how I stopped the next to the last hen, though she was impatient to go on. I inquired "Where are you all travelling?" She said "To Emporia." And so I asked, "Why are you swearing so?" She answered,

THE FIRST HARVEST

"Don't you know about the Sunday-school picnic?" I paused in my story.

No word from the Mennonites. One of them rose rather impatiently.

I poured some water on my head and continued: "I stopped the last hen. I asked: "Why are you swearing, sister? And what about the picnic?" She replied: "These Emporia people are going to give a Sunday-school picnic day after to-morrow. Meantime all us hens have to lay devilled eggs."

"We do not laugh at jokes about swearing," said the Mennonite driver, and climbed back on to his reaper. My partner strode solemnly out into the sun and began to pile sheaves.

Each round we study our shadows on the stubble more closely, thrilled with the feeling that noon creeps on. And now, up the road we see a bit of dust and a rig. No, it is not the woman we are looking for, but a woman with supplies for other harvesters. We work on and on, while four disappoint-

ing rigs go by.   At last appears a sunbonnet
we know.   Our especial Mennonite maid
is sitting quite straight on the edge of the
seat and holding the lines almost on a level
with her chin.   She drives through the field
toward us.   We motion her to the gap in the
hedge.

We unhitch, and lead the mules to the gap,
where she joins us.   With much high-mind-
ed expostulation the men try to show the
mules they should eat alfalfa and not hedge-
thorns.   The mules are at last tied out in the
sun to a wheel of the wagon, away from
temptation, with nothing but alfalfa near
them.

The meal is spread with delicacy, yet there
is a heap of it.   With a prayer of thanksgiving, sometimes said by Tilly, sometimes
by one of the men, we begin to eat.   To a
man in a harvest-field a square meal is more
thrilling than a finely-acted play.

The thrill goes not only to the toes and the
finger-tips, but to the utmost ramifications

of the spirit. Men indoors in offices, whose bodies actually require little, cannot think of eating enormously without thinking of sodden overeating, with condiments to rouse, and heavy meats and sweets to lull the flabby body till the last faint remnants of appetite have departed and the man is a monument of sleepy gluttony.

Eating in a harvest field is never so. Every nerve in the famished body calls frantically for reinforcements. And the nerves and soul of a man are strangely alert together. All we ate for breakfast turned to hot ashes in our hearts at eleven o'clock. I sing of the body and of the eternal soul, revived again! To feel life actually throbbing back into one's veins, life immense in passion, pulse and power, is not over-eating.

Tilly has brought us knives, and no forks. It would have been more appropriate if we had eaten from the ends of swords. We are finally recuperated from the fevers of the morning and almost strong enough for the long, long afternoon fight with the sun. Fresh water is poured from a big glittering can into the jugs we have sucked dry. Tilly reloads the buggy and is gone. After another sizzling douse of water without and within, our long afternoon pull commences.

The sun has become like a roaring lion, and we wrestle with the sheaves as though we had him by the beard. The only thing that keeps up my nerve in the dizziness is the remembrance of the old Mennonite's proverb at breakfast that as long as a man can eat and sweat he is safe. My hands inside my prickling gloves seem burning off. The wheat beards there are like red-hot needles. But I am still sweating a little in the chest, and the Mennonite boy is cheerfully singing:

> "When I behold the wondrous cross
> On which the Prince of Glory died,
> My richest gain I count but loss
> And pour contempt on all my pride."

THE FIRST HARVEST

Two-thirds round the field, methinks the jig is up. Then the sun is hidden by a friend of ours in the sky, just the tiniest sort of a cloud and we march on down the rows. The merciful little whiff of dream follows the sun for half an hour.

The most terrible heat is at half-past two. Somehow we pull through till four o'clock. Then we say to ourselves: "We can stand this four-o'clock heat, because we have stood it hotter."

'Tis a grim matter of comparison. We speed up a little and trot a little as the sun reaches the top of the western hedge. A bit later the religious hired man walks home to do the chores. I sing down the rows by myself. It is glorious to work now. The endless reiterations of the day have developed a certain dancing rhythm in one's nerves, one is intoxicated with his own weariness and the conceit that comes with seizing the sun by the mane, like Sampson.

It is now that the sun gracefully acknowledges his defeat. He shows through the hedge as a great blur, that is all. Then he becomes a mist-wrapped golden mountain that some fairy traveller might climb in enchanted shoes. This sun of ours is no longer an enemy, but a fantasy, a vision and a dream.

Now the elderly proprietor is back on his dancing pony. He is following the hurrying reaper in a sort of ceremonial fashion, delighted to see the wheat go down so fast. At last this particular field is done. We finish with a comic-tragedy. Some little rabbits scoot, panic-stricken, from the last few yards of still-standing grain. The old gentleman on horseback and his son afoot soon out-manœuvre the lively creatures. We have rabbit for supper at the sacrifice of considerable Mennonite calm.

It was with open rejoicing on the part of all that we finished the field nearest the house, the last one, by Saturday noon. The boy and I had our own special thrill in catching up with the reaper, which had passed by us so often in our rounds. As the square in mid-field grows smaller the reaper has to turn oftener, and turning uses up much more time than at first appears.

The places where the armies of wheat-sheaves are marshalled are magic places, despite their sweat and dust. There is nothing small in the panorama. All the lines of the scene are epic. The binder-twine is invisible, and has not altered the eternal classic form of the sheaf. There is a noble dignity and ease in the motion of a new reaper on a level field. A sturdy Mennonite devotee marching with a great bundle of wheat under each arm and reaching for a third makes a picture indeed, an essay on sunshine beyond the brush of any impressionist. Each returning day while riding to the field, when one has a bit of time to dream, one feels these things. One feels also the essentially partriarchal character of the harvest. One thinks of the Book of Ruth, and the Jewish

feasts of ingathering. All the new Testa-
ment parables ring in one's ears, parables of
sowing and reaping, of tares and good grain,
of Bread and of Leaven and the story of
the Disciples plucking corn. As one looks
on the half-gathered treasure he thinks on
the solemn words: "For the Bread of God
is that which cometh down out of Heaven
and giveth life unto the World," and the
rest of that sermon on the Bread of Life,
which has so many meanings.

This Sunday before breakfast, I could
fully enter into the daily prayers, that at
times had appeared merely quaint to me,
and in my heart I said "Amen" to the special
thanksgiving the patriarch lifted up for the
gift of the fruit of the land. I was happy
indeed that I had had the strength to bear
my little part in the harvest of a noble and
devout household, as well as a hand in the
feeding of the wide world.

What I, a stranger, have done in this
place, thirty thousand strangers are doing

just a little to the west. We poor tramps are helping to garner that which reestablishes the nations. If only for a little while, we have bent our backs over the splendid furrows, to save a shining gift that would otherwise rot, or vanish away.

THURSDAY AFTERNOON, JULY FOURTH, 1912. In the shadow of a lonely windmill between Raymond and Ellinwood, Kansas.

I arrived hot and ravenous at Raymond about eleven A.M. on this glorious Independence Day, having walked twelve miles facing a strange wind. At first it seemed fairly cool, because it travelled at the rate of an express train. But it was really hot and alkaline, and almost burnt me up. I had had for breakfast a cooky, some raisins and a piece of cheese, purchased with my booklet of rhymes at a grocery. By the time I reached Raymond I was fried and frantic.

The streets were deserted. I gathered from the station-master that almost everyone had gone to the Dutch picnic in the grove near Ellinwood. The returns for the Johnson-Flynn fight were to be received there beneath the trees, and a potent variety of dry-state beverage was to flow free. The unveracious station-master declared this beverage was made of equal parts iron-rust, patent medicine and rough-on-rats, added to a barrel of brown rain-water. He appeared to be prejudiced against it.

I walked down the street. Just as I had somehow anticipated, I spied out a certain type of man. He was alone in his restaurant and I crouched my soul to spring. The only man left in town is apt to be a soft-hearted party. "Here, as sure as my name is tramp, I will wrestle with a defenceless fellow-being."

Like many a restaurant in Kansas, it was a sort of farmhand's Saturday night paradise. If a man cannot loaf in a saloon he will loaf in a restaurant. Then certain problems of demand and supply arise according to circumstances and circumlocutions.

I obtained leave for the ice-water without wrestling. I almost emptied the tank. Then, with due art, I offered to recite twenty poems to the solitary man, a square meal to be furnished at the end, if the rhymes were sufficiently fascinating.

Assuming a judicial attitude on the lunch-counter stool he put me in the arm-chair by the ice-chest and told me to unwind myself. As usual, I began with *The Proud Farmer, The Illinois Village* and *The Building of Springfield,* which three in series contain my whole gospel, directly or by implication. Then I wandered on through all sorts of rhyme. He nodded his head like a mandarin, at the end of each recital. Then he began to get dinner. He said he liked my poetry, and he was glad I came in, for he would feel more like getting something to eat himself. I sat on and on by the ice-chest while he prepared a meal more heating

THE GOSPEL OF BEAUTY

than the morning wind or the smell of fire-crackers in the street. First, for each man, a slice of fried ham large enough for a whole family. Then French fried potatoes by the platterful. Then three fried eggs apiece. There was milk with cream on top to be poured from a big granite bucket as we desired it. There was a can of beans with tomato sauce. There was sweet apple-butter. There were canned apples. There was a pot of coffee. I moved over from the ice-chest and we talked and ate till half-past one. I began to feel that I was solid as an iron man and big as a Colossus of Rhodes. I would like to report our talk, but this letter must end somewhere. I agreed with my host's opinions on everything but the temperance question. He did not believe in *total* abstinence. On that I remained non-committal. Eating as I had, how could I take a stand against my benefactor even though the issue were the immortal one of man's sinful weakness for drink? The ham

THE FIRST HARVEST

and ice water were going to my head as it was. And I could have eaten more. I could have eaten a fat Shetland pony.

My host explained that he also travelled at times, but did not carry poetry. He gave me much box-car learning. Then, curious to relate, he dug out maps and papers, and showed me how to take up a claim in Oregon, a thing I did not in the least desire to do. God bless him in basket and in store, afoot or at home.

This afternoon the ham kept on frying within me, not uncomfortably. I stopped and drank at every windmill. Now it is about four o'clock in the afternoon and I am in the shadow of one more. I have found a bottle which just fits my hip pocket which I have washed and will use as a canteen henceforth. When one knows he has his drink with him, he does not get so thirsty.

But I have put down little to show you the strange intoxication that has pervaded this whole day. The inebriating character of the air and the water and the intoxication that comes with the very sight of the windmills spinning alone, and the elation that comes with the companionship of the sun, and the gentleness of the occasional good Samaritans, are not easily conveyed in words. When one's spirit is just right for this sort of thing it all makes as good an Independence Day as folks are having anywhere in this United States, even at Ellinwood.

THURSDAY, JULY 5, 1912. In the office of the Ellinwood livery stable in the morning.

Everyone came home drunk from the Dutch picnic last night. Ellinwood roared and Ellinwood snorted. I reached the place from the east just as the noisy revellers arrived from the south.

Ellinwood is an old German town full of bar-rooms, forced by the sentiment of the dry voters in surrounding territory to turn into restaurants, but only of late. The bar-

THE FIRST HARVEST

fixtures are defiantly retained. Ever and anon Ellinwood takes to the woods with malicious intent.

Many of the citizens were in a mad-dog fury because Flynn had not licked Johnson. This town seems to be of the opinion that that battle was important. The proprietor of the most fashionable hotel monopolized the 'phone on his return from the woods. He called up everybody in town. His conversation was always the same. "What'd ya think of the fight?" And without waiting for answer: "I'll bet one hundred thousand dollars that Flynn can lick Johnson in a fair fight. It's a disgrace to this nation that black rascal kin lay hands on a white man. I'll bet a hundred thousand dollars. . . . A hundred thousand dollars . .," etc.

I sat a long time waiting for him to get through. At last I put in my petition at another hostelrie. This host was intoxicated, but gentle. In exchange for what I call the

THE GOSPEL OF BEAUTY

squarest kind of a meal I recited the most
cooling verses I knew to a somewhat distracted, rather alcoholic company of harvest
hands. First I recited a poem in praise of
Lincoln and then one in praise of the up-
lifting influence of the village church. Then,
amid qualified applause, I distributed my
tracts, and retreated to this stable for the
night.

KANSAS

O, I have walked in Kansas
Through many a harvest field
And piled the sheaves of glory there
And down the wild rows reeled:

Each sheaf a little yellow sun,
A heap of hot-rayed gold;
Each binder like Creation's hand
To mould suns, as of old.

Straight overhead the orb of noon
Beat down with brimstone breath:
The desert wind from south and west
Was blistering flame and death.

THE FIRST HARVEST

Yet it was gay in Kansas,
A-fighting that strong sun;
And I and many a fellow-tramp
Defied that wind and won.

And we felt free in Kansas
From any sort of fear,
For thirty thousand tramps like us
There harvest every year.

She stretches arms for them to come,
She roars for helpers then,
And so it is in Kansas
That tramps, one month, are men.

We sang in burning Kansas
The songs of Sabbath-school,
The "Day Star" flashing in the East,
The "Vale of Eden" cool.

We sang in splendid Kansas
"The flag that set us free"—
That march of fifty thousand men
With Sherman to the sea.

We feasted high in Kansas
And had much milk and meat.
The tables groaned to give us power
Wherewith to save the wheat.

THE GOSPEL OF BEAUTY

Our beds were sweet alfalfa hay
Within the barn-loft wide.
The loft doors opened out upon
The endless wheat-field tide.

I loved to watch the wind-mills spin
And watch that big moon rise.
I dreamed and dreamed with lids half-shut,
The moonlight in my eyes.

For all men dream in Kansas
By noonday and by night,
By sunrise yellow, red and wild
And moonrise wild and white.

The wind would drive the glittering clouds,
The cottonwoods would croon,
And past the sheaves and through the leaves
Came whispers from the moon.

V

In Kansas: the Second and Third Harvest

TWO miles north of Great Bend. In the heart of the greatest wheat country in America, and in the midst of the harvest-time, Sunday, July 7, 1912.

I am meditating on the ways of Destiny. It seems to me I am here, not altogether by chance. But just why I am here, time must reveal.

Last Friday I had walked the ten miles from Ellinwood to Great Bend by 9 A.M. I went straight to the general delivery, where a package of tracts and two or three weeks' mail awaited me. I read about half through the letter-pile as I sat on a rickety bench in the public square. Some very loud-mouthed negroes were playing horse-shoe obstreperously. I began to wish Flynn had whipped Johnson. I was thinking of getting away from there, when two white men, evidently harvesters, sat down near me and diluted the color scheme.

One man said: "Harvest-wages this week are from two dollars and fifty cents up to four dollars. We are experienced men and worth three dollars and fifty cents." Then a German farmer came and negotiated with them in vain. He wanted to hold them down to three dollars apiece. He had his automobile to take his crew away that morning.

Then a fellow in citified clothes came to me and asked: "Can you follow a reaper and shock?" I said: *"Show me the wheat."* So far as I remember, it is the first time in my life anyone ever hunted me out and *asked* me to work for him. He put me into his buggy and drove me about two miles north to this place, just the region John Humphrey told me to find, though he did not specify this farm. I was offered $2.50 and keep, as the prophet foretold. The man who drove me out has put his place this year into the hands of a tenant who is my direct boss. I may not be able to last out, but all is well so far. I have made an acceptable hand, keeping up with the reaper by myself, and I feel something especial awaits me. But the reaper breaks down so often I do not know whether I can keep up with it without help when it begins going full-speed.

These people do not attend church like the Mennonites. The tenant wanted me to break the Sabbath and help him in the alfalfa to-day. He suggested that neither he nor I was so narrow-minded or superstitious as to be a "Sunday man." Besides he couldn't work the alfalfa at all without one more hand. I did not tell him so, but I felt I needed all Sunday to catch up on my tiredness. I suspect that my refusal to violate the Sabbath vexed him.

There has been a terrible row of some kind going on behind the barn all afternoon.

Maybe he is working off his vexation. At last the tenant's wife has gone out to "see about that racket." Now she comes in. She tells me they have been trying to break a horse.

The same farm, two miles north of Great Bend, July 8, 1912.

How many times in the counties further back I have asked with fear and misgiving for permission to work in the alfalfa, and have been repulsed when I confessed to the lack of experience! And now this morning I have pitched alfalfa hay with the best of them. We had to go to work early while the dew softened the leaves. It is a kind of clover. Once perfectly dry, the leaves crumble off when the hay is shaken. Then we must quit. The leaves are the nourishing part.

The owner of the place, the citified party who drove me out here the other day and who is generally back in town, was on top of that stack this morning, his collar off, his town shirt and pants somewhat the worse for the exertion. He puffed like a porpoise, for he was putting in place all the hay we men handed up to him. We lifted the alfalfa in a long bundle, using our three forks at one time. We worked like drilled soldiers, then went in to early dinner.

This is a short note written while the binder takes the necessary three turns round the new wheatfield that the tenant's brother and I are starting to conquer this afternoon. Three swaths of four bundles each must be cut, then I will start on my rounds, piling them into shocks of twelve bundles each.

I am right by the R. F. D. box that goes with this farm. I will put up the little tin flag that signals the postman. One of the four beasts hitched to the reaper is a broncho colt who came dancing to the field this afternoon, refusing to keep his head in line with the rest of the steeds, and, as a consequence, pulling the whole reaper. It transpires that

THE GOSPEL OF BEAUTY

the row in the horselot Sunday was caused
by this colt. He jumped up and left his
hoof-print on the chest of the man now driving him. So the two men tied him up and
beat him all afternoon with a double-tree,
cursing him between whacks, lashing themselves with Kansas whisky to keep up steam.
Yet he comes dancing to the field.

On the farm two miles north of Great
Bend, Wednesday evening, July 10, 1912.
I must write you a short note to-night
while the rest are getting ready for supper.
I will try to mail it to-morrow morning on
the way to the wheat. Let me assure you
that your letter will be heeded. I know
pretty well, by this time, what I can stand,
but if I feel the least bit unfit I will not go
into the sun. That is my understanding
with the tenant who runs the farm. I can
eat and sweat like a Mennonite. I sleep like
a top and wake up fresh as a little daisy.
So far I have gone dancing to the field as

THE SECOND HARVEST

the broncho did. But the broncho is a poor illustration. He is dead.

The broncho was the property of a little boy, the son of the man who owns the farm. The little boy had started with a lamb and raised it, then sold it for chickens, increasing his capital by trading and feeding till it was all concentrated to buy this colt. Then he and his people moved to town and left the colt, just at the breaking age, to be trained for a boy's pet by these men. Since he became obstreperous, they thought hitching him to the reaper would cure him, leaving a draught-horse in the barn to make place for the unruly one.

The tenant's brother, who drove the reaper, sent word to the little boy he had not the least idea what ailed Dick. He hinted to me later that whatever killed him must have come from some disease in his head.

Yes, it came from his head. That double-tree and that pitchfork handle probably missed his ribs once or twice and hit him somewhere around his eyes, in the course of the Sabbath afternoon services. Two whis- ky-lashed colt-breakers can do wonders with- out trying. I have been assured that this is the only way to subdue the beasts, that law and order must assert themselves or the whole barnyard will lead an industrial re- bellion. It is past supper now. I have been writing till the lamp is dim. I must go to my quilts in the hay.

To-day was the only time the reaper did not break down every half hour for repairs. So it was one continuous dance for me and my friend the broncho till about three o'clock in the afternoon, when the sun really did its best. Then the broncho went crazy. He shoved his head over the backs of two mules twice his size, and almost pushed them into the teeth of the sickle.

He was bleeding at the mouth and his eyes almost popped out of his head. He had hardly an inch of hide that was whole, and his raw places were completely covered with

THE SECOND HARVEST

Kansas flies. And the hot winds have made the flies so ravenous they draw blood from the back of the harvester's hand the moment they alight.

The broncho began to kick in all four directions at once. He did one good thing. He pulled the callouses off the hands of the tenant's brother, the driver, who still gripped the lines but surrendered his pride and yelled for me to help. I am as afraid of bronchos and mules as I am of buzz saws. Yet we separated the beasts somehow, the mules safely hitched to the fence, the broncho between us, held by two halter-ropes.

There was no reasoning with Dick. He was dying, and dying game. One of the small boys appeared just then and carried the alarm. Soon a more savage and indomitable man with a more eloquent tongue, the tenant himself, had my end of the rope. But not the most formidable cursing could stop Dick from bleeding at the mouth. Later the draught horse whose place he had taken was brought over from his pleasant rest in the barn and the two were tied head to head. The lordly tenant started to lead them toward home. But Dick fell down and died as soon as he reached a patch of unploughed prairie grass, which, I think, was the proper end for him. The peaceful draught horse was put in his place.

The reaper went back to work. The reaper cut splendidly the rest of this afternoon. As for me I never shocked wheat with such machine-like precision. I went at a dog-trot part of the time, and almost caught up with the machine.

The broncho should not have been called Dick. He should have been called Daniel Boone, or Davy Crockett or Custer or Richard, yes, Richard the Lion-Hearted. He came dancing to the field this morning, between the enormous overshadowing mules, and dancing feebly this noon. He pulled the whole reaper till three o'clock. I remember I asked the driver at noon what made the broncho dance. He answered: "The flies on his ribs, I suppose."

I fancy Dick danced because he was made to die dancing, just as the Spartans rejoiced and combed their long hair preparing to face certain death at Thermopylæ.

I think I want on my coat of arms a broncho, rampant.

THURSDAY, JULY 11, 1912. Great Bend, Kansas.

Yesterday I could lift three moderate-sized sheaves on the run. This morning I could hardly lift one, walking. This noon the foreman of the ranch, the man who, with his brother, disciplined the broncho, was furiously angry with me, because, as I plainly explained, I was getting too much sun and wanted a bit of a rest. He inquired, "Why didn't you tell me two days ago you were going to be overcome by the heat, so I could have had a man ready to take your place?" Also, "It's no wonder dirty homeless men are walking around the country looking for jobs." Also, a little later: "I have my opinion of any man on earth who is a quitter."

But I kept my serenity and told him that under certain circumstances I was apt to be a quitter, though, of course, I did not like to overdo the quitting business. I remained unruffled, as I say, and handed him and his brother copies of *The Gospel of Beauty* and *Rhymes to Be Traded for Bread* and bade them good-bye. Then I went to town and told the local editor on them for their horse-killing, which, I suppose, was two-faced of me.

The tenant's attitude was perfectly absurd. Hands are terribly scarce. A half day's delay in shocking that wheat would not have hurt it, or stopped the reaper, or altered any of the rest of the farm routine. He fired me without real hope of a substitute. I was working for rock-bottom wages and willing to have them docked all he

THE SECOND HARVEST

pleased if he would only give me six hours to catch up in my tiredness.

Anyway, here I am in the Saddlerock Hotel, to which I have paid in advance a bit of my wages, in exchange for one night's rest. I enclose the rest to you. I will start out on the road to-morrow, bathed, clean, dead broke and fancy free. I have made an effort to graduate from beggary into the respectable laboring class, which you have so often exhorted me to do.

I shall try for employment again, as soon as I rest up a bit. I enjoyed the wheat and the second-hand reaper, and the quaintness of my employers and all till the death of Richard the Lion-Hearted.

I am wondering whether I ought to be as bitter as I am against the horse-killers. We cannot have green fields just for bronchos to gambol in, or roads where they can trot unharnessed and nibble by the way. We must have Law and Order and Discipline.

But, thanks to the Good St. Francis who

marks out my path for me, I start to-morrow morning to trot unharnessed once again.

Sunday, July 14, 1912. In front of the
general store at Wright, Kansas, which
same is as small as a town can get.

I have been wondering why Destiny sent
me to that farm where the horse-killers flour-
ished. I suppose it was that Dick might
have at least one mourner. All the world's
heroes are heroes because they had the qualities of constancy and dancing gameness that
brought him to his death.

Some day I shall hunt up the right kind
of a Hindu and pay him filthy gold and
have him send the ghost of Dick to those
wretched men. They will be unable to move,
lying with eyes a-staring all night long.
Dreadful things will happen in that room,
dreadful things the Hindu shall devise after
I have told him what the broncho endured.
They shall wake in the morning, thinking it
all a dream till they behold the horse-shoe

prints all over the counterpane. Then they will try to sit up and find that their ribs are broken—well, I will leave it to the Hindu.

I have been waiting many hours at this town of Wright. To-day and yesterday I made seventy-six miles. Thirty-five of these miles I made yesterday in the automobile of the genial and scholarly Father A. P. Heimann of Kinsley, who took me as far as that point. I have been loafing here at Wright since about four in the afternoon. It is nearly dark now. Dozens of harvesters, already engaged for the week, have been hanging about and the two stores have kept open to accommodate them. There is a man to meet me here at eight o'clock. I may harvest for him four days. I told him I would not promise for longer. He has taken the train to a station further east to try to get some men for all week. If he does not return with a full quota he will take me on. While I am perfectly willing to work for two dollars and a half, many hold out for three.

The man I am waiting for overtook me two miles east of this place. He was hurrying to catch his train. He took me into his rig and made the bargain. He turned his horse over to me and raced for the last car as we neared the station. So here I am a few yards from the depot, in front of the general store, watching the horse of an utter stranger. Of course the horse isn't worth stealing, and his harness is half twine and wire. But the whole episode is so careless and free and Kansas-like.

Most of the crowd have gone, and I am awfully hungry. I might steal off the harness in the dark, and eat it. Somehow I have not quite the nerve to beg where I expect to harvest. I am afraid to try again in this fight with the sun, yet when a man overtakes me in the road and trusts me with his best steed and urges me to work for him, I hardly know how to refuse.

THE THIRD HARVEST

SUNDAY AFTERNOON, JULY 21, 1912. Loafing and dozing on my bed in the granary on the farm near Wright, Kansas, where I have been harvesting a full week.

The man I waited for last Sunday afternoon returned with his full quota of hands on the "Plug" train about nine o'clock. Where was I to sleep? I began to think about a lumber pile I had seen, when I discovered that five other farmers had climbed off that train. They were poking around in all the dark corners for men just like me. I engaged with a German named Louis Lix for the whole week, all the time shaking with misgivings from the memory of my last break-down. Here it is, Sunday, before I know it. Lix wants me back again next year, and is sorry I will not work longer. I have totalled about sixteen days of harvesting in Kansas, and though I sagged in the middle I think I have ended in fair style. Enclosed find all my wages except enough for one day's stay at Dodge City and three real hotel meals there—sherbet and cheese and crackers, and finger bowls at the end, and all such folly. Harvest eating is grand in its way but somehow lacks frills. Ah, if eating were as much in my letters as in my thoughts, this would be nothing but a series of menus!

I have helped Lix harvest barley, oats and wheat, mainly wheat. This is the world of wheat. In this genial region one can stand on a soap-box and see nothing else to the horizon. Walking the Santa Fé Trail beside the railroad means walking till the enormous wheat-elevator behind one disappears because of the curvature of the earth, like the ships in the geography picture, and walking on and on till finally in the west the top of another elevator appears, being gradually revealed because this earth is not flat like a table, but, as the geography says, curved like an apple or an orange.

In these fields, instead of working a reaper with a sickle eight feet long, they work a header with a twelve-foot sickle. Instead of four horses to this machine, there are six. Instead of one man or two following behind to the left of the driver to pile sheaves into shocks, a barge, a most copious slatted receptacle, drives right beside the header, catching the unbound wheat which is thrown up loosely by the machine. One pitchfork man in the barge spreads this cataract of headed wheat so a full load can be taken in. His partner guides the team, keeping precisely with the header.

But these two bargemen do not complete the outfit. Two others with their barge or "header-box" come up behind as soon as the first box starts over to the stack to be unloaded. Here the sixth man, the stacker, receives it, and piles it into a small mountain nicely calculated to resist cyclones. The green men are broken in as bargemen. The stacker is generally an old hand.

Unloading the wheat is the hardest part of the bargeman's work. His fork must

be full and he must be fast. Otherwise his
partner, who takes turns driving and filling, and who helps to pitch the wheat out,
will have more than half the pitching to do.
And all the time will be used up. Neither
man will have a rest-period while waiting
for the other barge to come up. This rest-
period is the thing toward which we all
wrestle. If we save it out we drink from
the water-jugs in the corner of the wagon.
We examine where the grasshoppers have
actually bitten little nicks out of our pitchfork handles, nicks that are apt to make
blisters. We tell our adventures and, when
the header breaks down, and must be
tinkered endlessly, and we have a grand
rest, the stacker sings a list of the most
amazing cowboy songs. He is a young man,
yet rode the range here for seven years before it became wheat-country. One day
when the songs had become hopelessly,
prosaically pornographic I yearned for a

change. I quoted the first stanza of Atalanta's chorus:

"When the hounds of Spring are on Winter's traces,
  The mother of months, in meadow or plain,
  Fills the shadows and windy places
  With lisp of leaves and ripple of rain——"

The stacker asked for more. I finished the chorus. Then I repeated it several times, while the header was being mended. We had to get to work. The next morning when my friend climbed into our barge to ride to the field he began:

" 'When the hounds of Spring are on Winter's traces,
  The mother of months, in meadow or plain,
  Fills the shadows——'

"Dammit, what's the rest of it? I've been trying to recite that piece all night."

Now he has the first four stanzas. And last evening he left for Dodge City to stay overnight and Sunday. He was resolved to purchase *Atalanta in Calydon* and find in the Public Library *The Lady of Shallot* and *The Blessed Damozel,* besides paying the usual visit to his wife and children.

Working in a header-barge is fun, more fun than shocking wheat, even when one is working for a Mennonite boss. The crew is larger. There is occasional leisure to be social. There is more cool wind, for one is higher in the air. There is variety in the work. One drives about a third of the time, guides the wheat into the header a third of the time and empties the barge a third of the time. The emptying was the backbreaking work.

And I was all the while fearful, lest, from plain awkwardness, or shaking from weariness, I should stick some man in the eye with my pitchfork. But I did not. I came nearer to being a real harvester every day. The last two days my hands were so hard I could work without gloves, this despite the way the grasshoppers had chewed the forkhandle.

THE THIRD HARVEST

Believe everything you have ever heard of the Kansas grasshoppers.

The heights of the header-barge are dramatically commanding. Kansas appears much larger than when we are merely standing in the field. We are just as high as upon a mountain-peak, for here, as there, we can see to the very edges of the eternities.

Now let me tell you of a new kind of weather.

Clouds thicken overhead. The wind turns suddenly cold. We shiver while we work. We are liable in five minutes to a hailstorm, a terrific cloudburst or a cyclone. The horses are unhitched. The barges are tied end to end. And *still* the barges may be blown away. They must be anchored even more safely. The long poles to lock the wheels are thrust under the bed through the spokes. It has actually been my duty to put this pole in the wheels every evening to keep the barges from being blown out of the barn-lot at night. Such is the accustomed weather excitement in Kansas. Just now we have excitement that is unusual. But as the storm is upon us it splits and passes to the north and south. There is not a drop of rain.

We are at work again in ten minutes. In two hours the sky is clear and the air is hot and alkaline. And ten thousand grasshoppers are glad to see that good old hot wind again, you may believe. They are preening themselves, each man in his place on the slats of the barge. They are enjoying their chewing tobacco the same as ever.

Wheat, wheat, wheat, wheat! States and continents and oceans and solar-systems of wheat! We poor ne'er-do-weels take our little part up there in the header half way between the sky and the earth, and in the evening going home, carrying Mister Stacker-Man in our barge, we sing *Sweet Rosy O'Grady* and the *Battle Hymn of the Republic*. And the most emphatic and unadulterated tramp among us harvesters, **a**

THE THIRD HARVEST

giant Swiss fifty years old, gives the yodel he learned when a boy.

This is a German Catholic family for which I have been working. We have had grace before and after every meal, and we crossed ourselves before and after every meal, except the Swiss, who left the table early to escape being blest too much.

My employers are good folk, good as the Mennonites. My boss was absolutely on the square all the week, as kind as a hard-working man has time to be. It gave me great satisfaction to go to Mass with him this morning. Though some folks talk against religion, though it sometimes appears to be a nuisance, after weighing all the evidence of late presented, I prefer a religious farmer.

THE GOSPEL OF BEAUTY

HERE'S TO THE SPIRIT OF FIRE

*Here's to the spirit of fire, wherever the flame is un-
furled,
In the sun, it may be, as a torch, to lead on and
enlighten the world;
That melted the glacial streams, in the day that no
memories reach,
That shimmered in amber and shell and weed on the
earliest beach;
The genius of love and of life, the power that will
ever abound,
That waits in the bones of the dead, who sleep till
the judgment shall sound.
Here's to the spirit of fire, when clothed in swift
music it comes,
The glow of the harvesting songs, the voice of the
national drums;
The whimsical, various fire, in the rhymes and ideas
of men,
Buried in books for an age, exploding and writhing
again,
And blown a red wind round the world, consuming
the lies in its mirth,
Then locked in dark volumes for long, and buried like
coal in the earth.
Here's to the comforting fire in the joys of the blind
and the meek,*

THE THIRD HARVEST

*In the customs of letterless lands, in the thoughts
   of the stupid and weak.*
*In the weariest legends they tell, in their cruellest,
   coldest belief,*
*In the proverbs of counter or till, in the arts of the
   priest or the thief.*
*Here's to the spirit of fire, that never the ocean can
   drown,*
*That glows in the phosphorent wave, and gleams in
   the sea-rose's crown;*
*That sleeps in the sunbeam and mist, that creeps as
   the wise can but know,*
*A wonder, an incense, a whim, a perfume, a fear and
   a glow,*
*Ensnaring the stars with a spell, and holding the
   earth in a net,*
*Yea, filling the nations with prayer, wherever man's
   pathway is set.*

VI

The End of the Road; Moonshine; and Some Proclamations

AUGUST 1, 1912. Standing up at the Postoffice desk, Pueblo, Colorado.

Several times since going over the Colorado border I have had such a cordial reception for the Gospel of Beauty that my faith in this method of propaganda is reawakened. I confess to feeling a new zeal. But there are other things I want to tell in this letter.

I have begged my way from Dodge City on, dead broke, and keeping all the rules of the road. I have been asked dozens of times by frantic farmers to help them at various tasks in western Kansas and eastern Colorado. I have regretfully refused all

THE END OF THE ROAD

but half-day jobs, having firmly resolved not to harvest again till I have well started upon a certain spiritual enterprise, namely, the writing of certain new poems that have taken possession of me in this high altitude, despite the physical stupidity that comes with strenuous walking. Thereby hangs a tale that I have not room for here.

Resolutely setting aside all recent wonders, I have still a few impressions of the wheatfield to record. Harvesting time in Kansas is such a distinctive institution! Whole villages that are dead any other season blossom with new rooming signs, fifty cents a room, or when two beds are in a room, twenty-five cents a bed. The eating counters are generally separate from these. The meals are almost uniformly twenty-five cents each. The fact that Kansas has no bar-rooms makes these shabby food-sodden places into near-taverns, the main assembly halls for men wanting to be hired, or those spending their coin. Famous villages where

an enormous amount of money changes
hands in wages and the sale of wheat-crops
are thus nothing but marvellous lines of
dirty restaurants. In front of the dingy
hotels are endless ancient chairs. Summer
after summer fidgety, sun-fevered, sticky
harvesters have gossiped from chair to chair
or walked toward the dirty band-stand in
the public square, sure, as of old, to be encountered by the anxious farmer, making
up his crew.

A few harvesters are seen, carrying their
own bedding; grasshopper bitten quilts with
all their colors flaunting and their cotton
gushing out, held together by a shawl-strap
or a rope. Almost every harvester has a
shabby suit-case of the paste-board variety
banging round his ankles. When wages are
rising the harvester, as I have said before,
holds out for the top price. The poor farmer
walks round and round the village half a
day before he consents to the three dollars.
Stacker's wages may be three to five simo-

leons and the obdurate farmer may have to consent to the five lest his wheat go to seed on the ground. It is a hard situation for a class that is constitutionally tightwad, often wisely so.

The roundhouses, water tanks, and all other places where men stealing freight rides are apt to pass, have enticing cards tacked on or near them by the agents of the mayors of the various towns, giving average wages, number of men wanted, and urging all harvesters good and true to come to some particular town between certain dates. The multitude of these little cards keeps the harvester on the alert, and, as the saying is: "Independent as a hog on ice."

To add to the farmer's distractions, still fresher news comes by word of mouth that three hundred men are wanted in a region two counties to the west, at fifty cents more a day. It sweeps through the harvesters' hotels, and there is a great banging of suitcases, and the whole town is rushing for the train. Then there is indeed a nabbing of men at the station, and sudden surrender on the part of the farmers, before it is too late.

Harvesting season is inevitably placarded and dated too soon in one part of the State, and not soon enough in another. Kansas weather does not produce its results on schedule. This makes not one, but many hurry-calls. It makes the real epic of the muscle-market.

Stand with me at the station. Behold the trains rushing by, hour after hour, freight-cars and palace cars of dishevelled men! The more elegant the equipage the more do they put their feet on the seats. Behold a saturnalia of chewing tobacco and sunburn and hairy chests, disturbing the primness and crispness of the Santa Fé, jostling the tourist and his lovely daughter.

They are a happy-go-lucky set. They have the reverse of the tightwad's vices. The harvester, alas, is harvested. Gamblers lie in wait for him. The scarlet woman has her pit digged and ready. It is fun for the police to lock him up and fine him. No doubt he often deserves it. I sat half an afternoon in one of these towns and heard the local undertaker tell horrible stories of friendless field hands with no kinsfolk anywhere discoverable, sunstruck and buried in a day or so by the county. One man's story he told in great detail. The fellow had complained of a headache, and left the field. He fell dead by the roadside on the way to the house. He was face downward in an ant hill. He was eaten into an unrecognizable mass before they found him at sunset. The undertaker expatiated on how hard it was to embalm such folks. It was a discourse marshalled with all the wealth of detail one reads in *The Facts in the Case of M. Valdemar.*

The harvester is indeed harvested. He gambles with sunstroke, disease and damnation. In one way or another the money trickles from his loose fingers, and he drifts from the wheat in Oklahoma north to the wheat in Nebraska. He goes to Canada to shock wheat there as the season recedes, and then, perhaps, turns on his tracks and makes for Duluth, Minnesota, we will say. He takes up lumbering. Or he may make a circuit of the late fruit crops of Colorado and California. He is, pretty largely, so much crude, loose, ungoverned human strength, more useful than wise. Looked at closely, he may be the boy from the machine-shop, impatient for ready money, the farmer failure turned farm-hand, the bank-clerk or machine-shop mechanic tired of slow pay, or the college student on a lark, in more or less incognito. He may be the intermittent criminal, the gay-cat or the travelling religious crank, or the futile tract-distributer.

And I was three times fraternally accosted by harvesters who thought my oilcloth package of poems was a kit of burglar's tools. It *is* a system of breaking in, I will admit.

A STORY LEFT OUT OF THE LETTERS

This ends the section of my letters home that in themselves make a consecutive story. But to finish with a bit of a nosegay, and show one of the unexpected rewards of troubadouring, let me tell the tale of the Five Little Children Eating Mush.

One should not be so vain as to recount a personal triumph. Still this is a personal triumph. And I shall tell it with all pride and vanity. Let those who dislike a conceited man drop the book right here.

I had walked all day straight west from Rocky Ford. It was pitch dark, threatening rain—the rain that never comes. It was nearly ten o'clock. At six I had entered a village, but had later resolved to press on to visit a man to whom I had a letter of introduction from my loyal friend Dr. Barbour of Rocky Ford.

There had been a wash-out. I had to walk around it, and was misdirected by the good villagers and was walking merrily on toward nowhere. Around nine o'clock I had been refused lodging at three different shanties. But from long experience I knew that something would turn up in a minute. And it did.

I walked right into the fat sides of a big country hotel on that interminable plain. It was not surrounded by a village. It was simply a clean hostelrie for the transient hands who worked at irrigating in that region.

I asked the looming figure I met in the dark: "Where is the boss of this place?"

"I am the boss." He had a Scandinavian twist to his tongue.

"I want a night's lodging. I will give in exchange an entertainment this evening, or half a day's work to-morrow."

THE END OF THE ROAD

"Come in."

I followed him up the outside stairway to the dining-room in the second story. There was his wife, a woman who greeted me cheerfully in the Scandinavian accent. She was laughing at her five little children who were laughing at her and eating their mush and milk.

Presumably the boarders had been delayed by their work, and had dined late. The children were at it still later.

They were real Americans, those little birds. And they had memories like parrots, as will appear.

"Wife," said the landlord, "here is a man that will entertain us to-night for his keep, or work for us to-morrow. I think we will take the entertainment to-night. Go ahead, mister. Here are the kids. Now listen, kids."

To come out of the fathomless, friendless dark and, almost in an instant, to look into such expectant fairy faces! They were

THE GOSPEL OF BEAUTY

laughing, laughing, laughing, not in mockery, but companionship. I recited every child-piece I had ever written—(not many).

They kept quite still till the end of each one. Then they pounded the table for more, with their tin spoons and their little red fists.

So, with misgivings, I began to recite some of my fairy-tales for grown-ups. I spoke slowly, to make the externals of each story plain. The audience squealed for more. . . . I decided to recite six jingles about the moon, that I had written long ago: How the Hyæna said the Moon was a Golden Skull, and how the Shepherd Dog contradicted him and said it was a Candle in the Sky—and all that and all that.

The success of the move was remarkable because I had never pleased either grown folks or children to any extent with those verses. But these children, through the accumulated excitements of a day that I knew

THE END OF THE ROAD

nothing about, were in an ecstatic imaginative condition of soul that transmuted everything.

The last of the series recounted what Grandpa Mouse said to the Little Mice on the Moon question. I arranged the ketchup bottle on the edge of the table for Grandpa Mouse. I used the salts and peppers for the little mice in circle round. I used a black hat or so for the swooping, mouse-eating owls that came down from the moon. Having acted out the story first, I recited it, slowly, mind you. Here it is:

WHAT GRANDPA MOUSE SAID

"The moon's a holy owl-queen:
　She keeps them in a jar
Under her arm till evening,
　Then sallies forth to war.

She pours the owls upon us:
　They hoot with horrid noise
And eat the naughty mousie-girls
　And wicked mousie-boys.

THE GOSPEL OF BEAUTY

So climb the moon-vine every night
And to the owl-queen pray:
Leave good green cheese by moonlit trees
For her to take away.

And never squeak, my children,
Nor gnaw the smoke-house door.
The owl-queen then will then love us
And send her birds no more."

At the end I asked for my room and retired. I slept maybe an hour. I was awakened by those tireless little rascals racing
along the dark hall and saying in horrible
solemn tones, pretending to scare one another:

"The moon's a holy owl-queen:
She keeps them in a jar
Under her arm till night,
Then 'allies out to war!
She sicks the owls upon us,
They 'OOT with 'orrid noise
And eat . . . the naughty boys,
And the MOON'S A HOLY OWL-QUEEN!
SHE KEEPS THEM IN A JAR!"

THE END OF THE ROAD

And so it went on, over and over.

Thereupon I made a mighty and a rash resolve. I renewed that same resolve in the morning when I woke. I said within myself *"I shall write one hundred Poems on the Moon!"*

Of course I did not keep my resolve to write one hundred pieces about the moon. But here are a few of those I did write immediately after:

THE FLUTE OF THE LONELY

[To the tune of Gaily the Troubadour.]

Faintly the ne'er-do-well
Breathed through his flute:
All the tired neighbor-folk,
Hearing, were mute.
In their neat doorways sat,
Labors all done,
Helpless, relaxed, o'er-wrought,
Evening begun.

None of them there beguiled
Work-thoughts away,

THE GOSPEL OF BEAUTY

Like to this reckless, wild
Loafer by day.
(Weeds in his flowers upgrown!
Fences awry!
Rubbish and bottles heaped!
Yard like a sty!)

There in his lonely door,
Leering and lean,
Staggering, liquor-stained,
Outlawed, obscene——
Played he his moonlight thought,
Mastered his flute.
All the tired neighbor-folk,
Hearing, were mute.
None but he, in that block,
Knew such a tune.
All loved the strain, and all
Looked at the moon!

THE SHIELD OF FAITH

The full moon is the Shield of Faith,
  And when it hangs on high
Another shield seems on my arm
  The hard world to defy.

THE END OF THE ROAD

Yea, when the moon has knighted me,
  Then every poisoned dart
Of daytime memory turns away
  From my dream-armored heart.

The full moon is the Shield of Faith:
  As long as it shall rise,
I know that Mystery comes again,
  That Wonder never dies.

I know that Shadow has its place,
  That Noon is not our goal,
That Heaven has non-official hours
  To soothe and mend the soul;

That witchcraft can be angel-craft
  And wizard deeds sublime;
That utmost darkness bears a flower,
  Though long the budding-time.

THE ROSE OF MIDNIGHT

[What the Gardener's Daughter Said]

The moon is now an opening flower,
  The sky a cliff of blue.
The moon is now a silver rose;
  Her pollen is the dew.

THE GOSPEL OF BEAUTY

Her pollen is the mist that swings
   Across her face of dreams:
Her pollen is the faint cold light
   That through the garden streams.

All earth is but a passion-flower
   With blood upon his crown.
And what shall fill his failing veins
   And lift his head, bowed down?

This cup of peace, this silver rose
   Bending with fairy breath
Shall lift that passion-flower, the earth,
   A million times from Death!

THE PATH IN THE SKY

I sailed a little shallop
Upon a pretty sea
In blue and hazy mountains,
Scarce mountains unto me;
Their summits lost in wonder,
They wrapped the lake around,
And when my shallop landed
I trod on a vague ground,

And climbed and climbed toward heaven,
Though scarce before my feet
I found one step unveiled there

THE END OF THE ROAD

The blue-haze vast, complete,
Until I came to Zion
The gravel paths of God:
My endless trail pierced the thick **veil**
To flaming flowers and sod.
I rested, looked behind me
And saw where I had been.
*My little lake. It was the **moon.***
Sky-mountains closed it in.

PROCLAMATIONS

Immediately upon my return from my journey the following Proclamations were printed in Farm and Fireside, through the great kindness of the editors, as another phase of the same crusade.

A PROCLAMATION
OF BALM IN GILEAD

GO to the fields, O city laborers, till your wounds are healed. Forget the streetcars, the skyscrapers, the slums, the Marseillaise song.

THE GOSPEL OF BEAUTY

We proclaim to the broken-hearted, still able to labor, the glories of the ploughed land. The harvests are wonderful. And there is a spiritual harvest appearing. A great agricultural flowering of art and song is destined soon to appear. Where corn and wheat are growing, men are singing the psalms of David, not the Marseillaise.

You to whom the universe has become a blast-furnace, a coke-oven, a cinder-strewn freight-yard, to whom the history of all ages is a tragedy with the climax now, to whom our democracy and our flag are but play-things of the hypocrite,—turn to the soil, turn to the earth, your mother, and she will comfort you. Rest, be it ever so little, from your black broodings. Think with the farmer once more, as your fathers did. Revere with the farmer our centuries-old civilization, however little it meets the city's trouble. Revere the rural customs that have their roots in the immemorial benefits of nature.

THE END OF THE ROAD

With the farmer look again upon the Constitution as something brought by Providence, prepared for by the ages. Go to church, the cross-roads church, and say the Lord's Prayer again. Help them with their temperance crusade. It is a deeper matter than you think. Listen to the laughter of the farmer's children. Know that not all the earth is a-weeping. Know that so long as there is black soil deep on the prairie, so long as grass will grow on it, we have a vast green haven.

The roots of some of our trees are still in the earth. Our mountains need not to be moved from their places. Wherever there is tillable land, there is a budding and blooming of old-fashioned Americanism, which the farmer is making splendid for us against the better day.

There is perpetual balm in Gilead, and many city workmen shall turn to it and be healed. This by faith, and a study of the signs, we proclaim!

THE GOSPEL OF BEAUTY

PROCLAMATION

Of the New Time for Farmers and the New New England

LET it be proclaimed and shouted over all the ploughlands of the United States that the same ripening that brought our first culture in New England one hundred years ago is taking place in America to-day. Every State is to have its Emerson, its Whittier, its Longfellow, its Hawthorne and the rest.

Our Puritan farmer fathers in our worthiest handful of States waited long for their first group of burnished, burning lamps. From the landing of the Pilgrims in 1620 to the delivery of Emerson's address on the American Scholar was a weary period of gestation well rewarded.

Therefore, let us be thankful that we have come so soon to the edge of this occasion, that the western farms, though scarcely settled, have the Chautauqua, which is New England's old rural lecture course; the temperance crusade, which is New England's abolitionism come again; the magazine militant, which is the old Atlantic Monthly combined with the Free-Soil Newspaper under a new dress, and educational reform, which is the Yankee school-house made glorious.

All these, and more, electrify the farmlands. Things are in that ferment where many-sided Life and Thought are born.

Because our West and South are richer and broader and deeper than New England, so much more worth while will our work be. We will come nearer to repeating the spirit of the best splendors of the old Italian villages than to multiplying the prunes and prisms of Boston.

The mystery-seeking, beauty-serving followers of Poe in their very revolt from democracy will serve it well. The Pan-worshipping disciples of Whitman will in the end be, perhaps, more useful brothers of the

White Christ than all our coming saints.
And men will not be infatuated by the written and spoken word only, as in New England. Every art shall have the finest devotion.

Already in this more tropical California, this airier Colorado, this black-soiled Illinois, in Georgia, with her fire-hearted tradition of chivalry and her new and most romantic prosperity, men have learned to pray to the God of the blossoming world, men have learned to pray to the God of Beauty. They meditate upon His ways. They have begun to sing.

As of old, their thoughts and songs begin with the land, and go directly back to the land. Their tap-roots are deep as those of the alfalfa. A new New England is coming, a New England of ninety million souls! An artistic Renaissance is coming. An America is coming such as was long ago prophesied in Emerson's address on the

American Scholar. This by faith, and a study of the signs, we proclaim!

PROCLAMATION

Of the New Village, and the New Country Community, as Distinct from the Village

THIS is a year of bumper crops, of harvesting festivals. Through the mists of the happy waning year, a new village rises, and the new country community, in visions revealed to the rejoicing heart of faith.

And yet it needs no vision to see them. Walking across this land I have found them, little ganglions of life, promise of thousands more. The next generation will be that of the eminent village. The son of the farmer will be no longer dazzled and destroyed by the fires of the metropolis. He will travel, but only for what he can bring back. Just as his father sends half-way across the continent for good corn, or melon-seed, so he will make his village famous by transplanting and growing this idea or that. He will make it known for its pottery or its processions, its philosophy or its pea-cocks, its music or its swans, its golden roofs or its great union cathedral of all faiths. There are a thousand miscellaneous achievements within the scope of the great-hearted village. Our agricultural land to-day holds the ploughboys who will bring these benefits. I have talked to these boys. I know them. I have seen their gleaming eyes.

And the lonely country neighborhood, as distinct from the village, shall make itself famous. There are river valleys that will be known all over the land for their tall men and their milk-white maidens, as now for their well-bred horses. There are mountain lands that shall cultivate the tree of knowl-edge, as well as the apple-tree. There are sandy tracts that shall constantly ripen red and golden citrus fruit, but as well, philosophers comforting as the moon, and strength-giving as the sun.

These communities shall have their proud circles. They shall have families joined hand in hand, to the end that new blood and new thoughts be constantly brought in, and no good force or leaven be lost. The country community shall awaken illustrious. This by faith, and a study of the signs, we proclaim!

PROCLAMATION

Welcoming the Talented Children of the Soil

BECAUSE of their closeness to the earth, the men on the farms increase in stature and strength.

And for this very reason a certain proportion of their children are being born with a finer strength. They are being born with all this power concentrated in their nerves.

THE GOSPEL OF BEAUTY

They have the magnificent thoughts that might stir the stars in their courses, were they given voice.

Yea, in almost every ranch-house is born one flower-like girl or boy, a stranger among the brothers and sisters. Welcome, and a thousand welcomes, to these fairy change-lings! They will make our land lovely. Let all of us who love God give our hearts to these His servants. They are born with eyes that weep themselves blind, unless there is beauty to look upon. They are endowed with souls that are self-devouring, unless they be permitted to make rare music; with a desire for truth that will make them mad as the old prophets, unless they be permitted to preach and pray and praise God in their own fashion, each establishing his own dream visibly in the world.

The land is being jewelled with talented children, from Maine to California: souls dewy as the grass, eyes wondering and passionate, lips that tremble. Though they be born in hovels, they have slender hands, seemingly lost amid the heavy hands. They have hands that give way too soon amid the bitter days of labor, but are everlastingly patient with the violin, or chisel, or brush, or pen.

All these children as a sacred charge are appearing, coming down upon the earth like manna. Yet many will be neglected as the too-abundant mulberry, that is left upon the trees. Many will perish like the wild strawberries of Kansas, cut down by the roadside with the weeds. Many will be looked upon like an over-abundant crop of apples, too cheap to be hauled to market, often used as food for the beasts. There will be a great slaughter of the innocents, more bloody than that of Herod of old. But there will be a desperate hardy remnant, adepts in all the conquering necromancy of agricultural Song and democratic Craftsmanship. They will bring us our new time in its completeness.

THE GOSPEL OF BEAUTY

This by faith, and a study of the signs, we proclaim!

PROCLAMATION

Of the Coming of Religion, Equality and Beauty

IN OUR new day, so soon upon us, for the first time in the history of Democracy, art and the church shall be hand in hand and equally at our service. Neither craftsmanship nor prayer shall be purely aristocratic any more, nor at war with each other, nor at war with the State. The priest, the statesman and the singer shall discern one another's work more perfectly and give thanks to God.

Even now our best churches are blossoming in beauty. Our best political life, whatever the howlers may say, is tending toward equality, beauty and holiness.

Political speech will cease to turn only upon the price of grain, but begin considering the price of cross-roads fountains and people's palaces. Our religious life will no longer trouble itself with the squabbles of orthodoxy. It will give us the outdoor choral procession, the ceremony of dedicating the wheat-field or the new-built private house to God. That politician who would benefit the people will not consider all the world wrapped up in the defence or destruction of a tariff schedule. He will serve the public as did Pericles, with the world's greatest dramas. He will rebuild the local Acropolis. He will make his particular Athens rule by wisdom and philosophy, not trade alone. Our crowds shall be audiences, not hurrying mobs; dancers, not brawlers; observers, not restless curiosity-seekers. Our mobs shall becomes assemblies and our assemblies religious; devout in a subtle sense, equal in privilege and courtesy, delicate of spirit, a perfectly rounded democracy.

All this shall come through the services of three kinds of men in wise coöperation: the priests, the statesmen and the artists. Our priests shall be religious men like St. Francis, or John Wesley, or General Booth, or Cardinal Newman. They shall be many types, but supreme of their type.

Our statesmen shall find their exemplars and their inspiration in Washington, Jefferson and Lincoln, as all good Americans devoutly desire.

But even these cannot ripen the land without the work of men as versatile as William Morris or Leonardo. Our artists shall fuse the work of these other workers, and give expression to the whole cry and the whole weeping and rejoicing of the land. We shall have Shelleys with a heart for religion, Ruskins with a comprehension of equality.

Religion, equality and *beauty!* By these America shall come into a glory that shall justify the yearning of the sages for her perfection, and the prophecies of the poets, when she was born in the throes of Valley Forge.

THE END OF THE ROAD

This, by faith, and a study of the signs,
we proclaim!

EPILOGUE

[*Written to all young lovers about to set up homes*
of their own—but especially to those of some
far-distant day, and those of my home-village]

Lovers, O lovers, listen to my call.
  Give me kind thoughts. I woo you on my knees.
Lovers, pale lovers, when the wheat grows tall,
  When willow trees are Eden's incense trees:—

I would be welcome as the rose in flower
  Or busy bird in your most secret fane.
I would be read in your transcendent hour
  When book and rhyme seem for the most part vain.

I would be read, the while you kiss and pray.
  I would be read, ere the betrothal ring
Circles the slender finger and you say
  Words out of Heaven, while your pulses sing.

O lovers, be my partisans and build
  Each home with a great fire-place as is meet.
When there you stand, with royal wonder filled,
  In bridal peace, and comradeship complete,

THE GOSPEL OF BEAUTY

While each dear heart beats like a fairy drum—
 Then burn a new-ripe wheat-sheaf in my name.
Out of the fire my spirit-bread shall come
 And my soul's gospel swirl from that red flame.

THE
VILLAGE IMPROVEMENT
PARADE

THE VILLAGE IMPROVEMENT
PARADE. SECTION I.

NICHOLAS
VACHEL 1910.
LINDSAY

THE
VILLAGE
IMPROVEMENT
PARADE
SECTION II.

225

A HASTY PROSPERITY MAY BE RAW AND ABSURD: A WELL-CONSIDERED POVERTY MAY BE EXQUISITE.

WITHOUT AN EAGER PUBLIC ALL TEACHING IS VAIN.

THE VILLAGE IMPROVEMENT PARADE.
SECTION III.

NICHOLAS
VACHEL 1910.
LINDSAY

THE VILLAGE IMPROVEMENT
PARADE SECTION IV.

NICHOLAS
VACHEL
LINDSAY
1910

OUR BEST SHOULD
PICTURES SHOULD
BE GOOD PAINTING
OUR BEST
MONUMENTS
SHOULD BE REAL
SCULPTURE
OUR BEST BUILDINGS
SHOULD BE REAL
ARCHITECTURE

UGLINESS
IS A KIND
OF MIS-
GOVERNMENT

THE VILLAGE
IMPROVEMENT
PARADE
SECTION V.

FAIR STREETS ARE
BETTER THAN SILVER
GREEN PARKS ARE
BETTER THAN
GOLD

BAD PUBLIC
TASTE IS MOB
LAW
GOOD PUBLIC
TASTE IS
DEMOCRACY

TO BEGIN, WE
MUST HAVE A
SENSE OF
HUMOR
AND LEARN
TO SMILE

THE VILLAGE
IMPROVEMENT PARADE
SECTION VI

NICHOLAS
VACHEL
LINDSAY
1910

RHYMES TO BE TRADED FOR BREAD

BEING NEW VERSES BY NICHOLAS VACHEL LINDSAY, SPRINGFIELD, ILLINOIS, JUNE, 1912. PRINTED EXPRESSLY AS A SUBSTITUTE FOR MONEY.

THIS BOOK IS TO BE USED IN EXCHANGE FOR THE NECESSITIES OF LIFE ON A TRAMP-JOURNEY FROM THE AUTHOR'S HOME TOWN, THROUGH THE WEST AND BACK, DURING WHICH HE WILL OBSERVE THE FOLLOWING RULES: (1) KEEP AWAY FROM THE CITIES. (2) KEEP AWAY FROM THE RAILROADS. (3) HAVE NOTHING TO DO WITH MONEY. CARRY NO BAGGAGE. (4) ASK FOR DINNER ABOUT QUARTER AFTER ELEVEN. (5) ASK FOR SUPPER, LODGING AND BREAKFAST ABOUT QUARTER OF FIVE. (6) TRAVEL ALONE. (7) BE NEAT, TRUTHFUL, CIVIL AND ON THE SQUARE. (8) PREACH THE GOSPEL OF BEAUTY.

IN ORDER TO CARRY OUT THE LAST RULE THERE WILL BE THREE EXCEPTIONS TO THE RULE AGAINST BAGGAGE. (1) THE AUTHOR WILL CARRY A BRIEF PRINTED STATEMENT, CALLED "THE GOSPEL OF BEAUTY." (2) HE WILL CARRY THIS BOOK OF RHYMES FOR DISTRIBUTION. (3) ALSO HE WILL CARRY A SMALL PORTFOLIO WITH PICTURES, ETC., CHOSEN TO GIVE AN OUTLINE OF HIS VIEW OF THE HISTORY OF ART, ESPECIALLY AS IT APPLIES TO AMERICA.

INTRODUCTION

UPON RETURNING TO THE COUNTRY ROAD.

EVEN THE SHREWD AND BITTER,
GNARLED BY THE OLD WORLD'S GREED,
CHERISHED THE STRANGER SOFTLY
SEEING HIS UTTER NEED.
SHELTER AND PATIENT HEARING,
THESE WERE THEIR GIFTS TO HIM,
TO THE MINSTREL GRIMLY BEGGING
AS THE SUNSET-FIRE GREW DIM.
THE RICH SAID "YOU ARE WELCOME."
YEA, EVEN THE RICH WERE GOOD.
HOW STRANGE THAT IN THEIR FEASTING
HIS SONGS WERE UNDERSTOOD!
THE DOORS OF THE POOR WERE OPEN,
THE POOR WHO HAD WANDERED TOO,
WHO HAD SLEPT WITH NE'ER A ROOF-TREE
UNDER THE WIND AND DEW.
THE MINDS OF THE POOR WERE OPEN,
THERE DARK MISTRUST WAS DEAD.
THEY LOVED HIS WIZARD STORIES,
THEY BOUGHT HIS RHYMES WITH BREAD.
THOSE WERE HIS DAYS OF GLORY,
OF FAITH IN HIS FELLOW-MEN.
THEREFORE, TODAY THE SINGER   .. ..
TURNS BEGGAR ONCE AGAIN.

HE BLEW ME TO A WINDLAND BUSH;
WITH SPEED AND JOY WE FLEW.
THE GREAT BUSH BLOOMED WITH PARCH-MENTS FINE, OF SONGS THAT FEED THE SOUL,
ALL NEW, THAT OUR DEAR EARTH SHALL HEAR, WHEN POETS REACH THEIR GOAL.
WHEN OUR GROWN CHILDREN, BREATHING FIRE, SHALL JUSTIFY ALL TIME,
BY HYMNS OF LIVING SILVER, SONGS WITH SUNRISE IN THE RHYME.
I WISH THAT I HAD LEARNED BY HEART SOME LYRICS READ THAT DAY,
I KNEW NOT 'TWAS A GIANT HOUR, AND SPENT IT ALL IN PLAY.

WINDLAND GLEAMS SO DEWY-WHITE, SO FULL OF CRYSTAL PEACE,
AND EVERY LEAF A SILKEN HARP, WHOSE MURMURS WILL NOT CEASE.
I GORGED THE HONEY FROM THE CUPS OF WILD-FLOWERS ALL ABOUT,
LAUGHING WHEN THE WIZARD LAUGHED, AND PUT THE GNATS TO ROUT.
I READ ONCE MORE, THEN SLEPT AWHILE, THEN WOKE ON EARTH AGAIN,
I WISH THOSE SCROLLS WERE MINE THAT I MIGHT BRING THEM UNTO MEN!

VERSES OF FANTASY AND DESIRE

THE WIZARD WIND.

THE WIZARD WIND'S A FRIEND OF MINE,—
MOST INTIMATE, IN TRUTH,
HE WHISTLES SORROW HALF AWAY, HE GIVES ME GOLDEN YOUTH.
AND FREE AS THAT SMALL BIRD THAT EATS THE WHEAT-EAR IN THE SHEAF
I AM NO LONGER MAN, BUT CLOUD, OR TUMBLED MAPLE-LEAF.
ONCE HE TRANSFORMED ME TO A BEE, HUNGRY FOR HONEY-DEW,

THE KING OF YELLOW BUTTER-FLIES.

(EARLY SPRING.)

THE KING OF YELLOW BUTTERFLIES NOW ORDERS FORTH HIS MEN,
HE SAYS, "THE TIME IS ALMOST HERE WHEN VIOLETS BLOOM AGAIN."
ADOWN THE ROAD THE FICKLE ROUT GOES FLASHING PROUD AND BOLD,
THEY SHIVER BY THE SHALLOW POOLS AND WHIMPER OF THE COLD.
THEY DRINK AND DRINK. 'TIS A PRE-TENCE. THEY LOVE TO POSE AND PREEN,

EACH POOL IS BUT A LOOKING-GLASS
    WHERE THEIR SWEET WINGS ARE
    SEEN.
THEY'RE GENTLEMEN — ADVENTURERS,
    THEY'RE GIPSIES EVERY WHIT,
THEY LIVE ON WHAT THEY STEAL. THEIR
    WINGS BY BRIARS ARE FRAYED A BIT.
THEIR LOVES ARE LIGHT. THEY HAVE NO
    HOUSE. AND IF IT RAINS TODAY
THEY'LL CLIMB INTO YOUR CATTLE-SHED,
    AND HIDE THEM IN THE HAY.

THE GRAVE OF THE RIGHTEOUS KITTEN.

HERE LIES A KITTEN GOOD, WHO KEPT
A KITTEN'S PROPER PLACE.
HE STOLE NO PANTRY EATABLES,
NOR SCRATCHED THE BABY'S FACE.
HE LET THE ALLEY-CATS ALONE,
HE HAD NO YOWLING VICE.
HIS SHIRT WAS ALWAYS LAUNDRIED WELL,
HE FREED THE HOUSE OF MICE.
UNTIL HIS DEATH HE HAD NOT CAUSED
HIS LITTLE MISTRESS TEARS,
HE WORE HIS RIBBON PRETTILY,
HE WASHED BEHIND HIS EARS.

AN INDIAN SUMMER DAY ON THE PRAIRIE.

(IN THE BEGINNING.)
THE SUN IS A HUNTRESS YOUNG,
THE SUN IS A RED, RED JOY,
THE SUN IS AN INDIAN GIRL,
OF THE TRIBE OF THE ILLINOIS.
    (MID-MORNING.)
THE SUN IS A SMOULDERING FIRE,
THAT CREEPS THROUGH THE HIGH GREY
    PLAIN
AND LEAVES NOT A BUSH OF CLOUD
TO BLOSSOM WITH FLOWERS OF RAIN.
    (NOON.)
THE SUN IS A WOUNDED DEER,
THAT TREADS PALE GRASS IN THE SKIES.
SHAKING HIS GOLDEN HORNS,
FLASHING HIS BALEFUL EYES.
    (SUNSET.)
THE SUN IS AN EAGLE OLD,
THERE IN THE WINDLESS WEST
ATOP OF THE SPIRIT-CLIFFS
HE BUILDS HIM A CRIMSON NEST.

WHY I FLED FROM DUTY.

I HAVE LOST YOU, LITTLE MISS DUTY.
I TOLD YOU MY LUST AND LOVE,
LUST LIKE THE PULSE OF THE TIGER—
THE HUNGER OF HAWK FOR DOVE.
I HAVE LOST YOU, LITTLE MISS DUTY,
THOUGH I BROUGHT YOU MYSELF QUITE
    WHOLE,
WHITE BODY AND BLACK DESIRE—
CONSCIENCE, AND BREATH, AND SOUL.
"YOU ARE NAKED," SAID LITTLE MISS
    DUTY,
"GO HIDE IN THE CAVES AND HILLS,
FOR I MUST BE GILDING COBWEBS,
I AM CHAINED IN THE COBWEB MILLS.

MY SILK BUYS BREAD AND BUTTER
AND PAYS MY DEBT ON THE FARM."
SO I STOLE HER SHOE FOR REMEMBERANCE
AND FLED LEST I DO HER HARM.

MACHINERY.

OH, EGYPT—QUEEN OF EGYPT—
WHEN I WAS KING OF BIRDS
YOU CALLED ME FROM THE TREETOPS
WITH MYSTIC COPTIC WORDS.
YOU WHISTLED AND YOU WHISPERED,
THEN MOCKED ME, FICKLE QUEEN.
YOU SAID TO ALL MY SOUL TALK:
"A BIRD IS A MACHINE."
YOUR TRIBE WAS OLD IN SCIENCE
YOU SAID TO ME—"YOUR WINGS
ARE RODS AND STRINGS AND HINGES;
THE PLACE IN YOU THAT SINGS.
"IS A TINY WILLOW WHISTLE,
QUITE WELL DEVISED, BUT STILL
A SISTRUM MAKES MORE MUSIC:
A FEATHER'S BUT A QUILL;
"A CLAW IS BUT A NEEDLE:
A CRAW, A MILL FOR CORN;
YOUR HEART IS BUT A LITTLE PUMP,
YOUR SOUL WAS NEVER BORN."

BUT THEN, I SANG SO DESPERATELY . . . .
I MADE FAIR EGYPT SIGH:—
"OH DOWNY SOUL IMMORTAL!
OH BIRD THAT CANNOT DIE!"

LOVE AND LAW.

TRUE LOVE IS FOUNDED IN ROCKS OF RE-
    MEMBERANCE,
IN STONES OF FORBEARANCE AND MORTAR
    OF PAIN.
THE WORKMAN LAYS WEARILY GRANITE
    ON GRANITE,
AND BLEEDS FOR HIS CASTLE 'MID SUN-
    SHINE AND RAIN.
LOVE IS NOT VELVET, NOT ALL OF IT VEL-
    VET,
NOT ALL OF IT BANNERS, NOT GOLD-LEAF
    ALONE.
'TIS STERN AS THE AGES, AND OLD AS
    RELIGION,
WITH PATIENCE ITS WATCHWORD AND
    LAW FOR ITS THRONE.

THE FLIGHT OF MONA LISA.

BEING THE SECRET HISTORY OF THE
STEALING OF LEONARDO DA VINCI'S MAS-
TERPIECE FROM THE GALLERY OF THE
LOUVRE.

ALWAYS ENTHRONED, AND EVER WISE AND
    STILL * * *
RIVERS OF STARING, STRENUOUS FOLK
    WENT BY.
ONLY THE WISE AND RIPE OF SOUL
    WOULD PAUSE,
MARKING THE SHADOWED MAGIC OF YOUR
    EYE * * *
NOW MOBS UNDO YOUR NAME WITH
    CLACKING TONGUE.
TOO DULL TO KNOW THE LADY THAT YOU
    ARE,

IGNORANT OF THE RENAISSANCE SO SWEET
OF WHICH YOU WERE THE CULMINATING
STAR—
CROWDS, TO WHOM BEAUTY IS A HIDDEN
BOOK—
THOUGH THEY GO SEEK IT TILL THEIR
EYES ARE RED;
MEN TO WHOM LEONARDO IS UNKNOWN
OR BUT A DUSTY FAME, A LONG TIME
DEAD:
THESE SAY THAT YOU WERE COURTED BY
A THIEF,
NAY, RATHER, AFTER HALF A THOUSAND
YEARS,
YOUR SMILE TOOK ON AN UNEXPECTED
BLOOM,
DESIRE AROSE THAT MOVED YOU NIGH TO
TEARS.
YOU FLASHED THAT PRINCESS-GLANCE
THAT WAS COMMAND—
"CARRY ME WITH YOU YOUTH. I LEAVE
THIS PLACE.
I GROW LOVE-HUNGRY 'MID THE CEN-
TURIES,
YOURS IS THE DESTINED, FLUSHED ADOR-
ING FACE!"
AH, WHAT A BEAUTEOUS, WICKED THING
IT WAS,
THIS RECKLESS HOPE OF YOURS THAT
STUNG HIM SO—
TILL, SCORNING YOUR FAIR PALACE AND
YOUR GUARD,
HE HALED YOU TO SOME LONELY PLACE
AGLOW.
WHY DID THIS SUDDEN THIRST OF YOURS
AWAKE?
CAN FEVER MUTINY IN VEINS SO OLD?
WHAT, IN HIS GESTURE TAMED YOUR
SPIRIT HIGH?
WHAT, IN HIS FIGURE MADE YOUR
GLANCES BOLD?
TILL, DAY BY DAY YOUR LONG LOOK
WITCHING HIM,
HIS FLAGGING PULSES KINDLED TO SPICED
FIRE,
AND REACHED AT LAST THE RENAISSANCE
SUPREME
ATTAINED THE HEIGHT OF FLORENTINE
DESIRE?
I KNOW 'TWAS LEONARDO COME TO EARTH
IN MASQUERADING FANCY DRESSED SO
GAY.
TRANSFORMED INTO A CARELESS ARTIST-
BOY,
A LOAFING STUDENT WASTING OUT THE
DAY.
AH, GROWN SO WEARY OF HIGH HEAVEN'S
STREETS!
AND OF THE GLITTERING SAINTS TOO-
RIGHTEOUS GRACE!
WEARY OF GODLY SUNSHINE WITHOUT
END!
SEEKING AGAIN THE SHADOWS OF YOUR
FACE!
YOU DID NOT KNOW HIM FOR HIMSELF
UNTIL
YOU FLED, WITHIN HIS ARMS, ADOWN
THE STAIR,

THEN, (AND YOU SAW THE GLEAMING
PARIS STREET),
HE STOOD A GREY WISE MAN BESIDE YOU
THERE.
A WANDERING JEW, TO YOU HIS HEART'S
OLD HOME,
HE CAME, AND GAVE YOUR SOUL AT LAST
SURPRISE,
HE STRANGELY BROUGHT A CHILD-ASTON-
ISHMENT,
A NOBLE MAIDEN-WONDER TO YOUR EYES.
HE RAVISHED YOU AWAY TO HEAVEN
WITH HIM,
STILL YEARNING FOR YOUR BITTER KISS
AGAIN—
YOUR BITTER, GENTLE, DOVE-LIKE WEARI-
NESS,
AND FOLLIES GARNERED 'MID THE SONS
OF MEN.

AN APOLOGY FOR THE BOTTLE
VOLCANIC.

SOMETIMES I DIP MY PEN AND FIND THE
BOTTLE FULL OF FIRE,
THE SALAMANDERS FLYING FORTH I CAN-
NOT BUT ADMIRE.
ITS ETNA, OR VESUVIUS, IF THOSE BIG
THINGS WERE SMALL,
AND THEN 'TIS BUT ITSELF AGAIN, AND
DOES NOT SMOKE AT ALL.
AND SO MY BLOOD GROWS COLD. I SAY,
"THE BOTTLE HELD BUT INK,
AND, IF YOU THOUGHT IT OTHERWISE,
THE WORSER FOR YOUR THINK.."
AND THEN, JUST AS I THROW MY SCRIB-
BLED PAPER ON THE FLOOR
THE BOTTLE SAYS "FE, FI, FO, FUM," AND
STEAMS AND SHOUTS SOME MORE.
OH, SAD DECEIVING INK, AS BAD AS LIQUOR
IN ITS WAY—
ALL DEMONS OF A BOTTLE SIZE HAVE
PRANCED FROM YOU TODAY,
AND SEIZED MY PEN FOR HOBBY-HORSE
AS WITCHES RIDE A BROOM,
AND LEFT A TRAIL OF BRIMSTONE WORDS
AND BLOTS AND GOBS OF GLOOM.
AND YET WHEN I AM EXTRA GOOD AND
SAY MY PRAYERS AT NIGHT,
AND MIND MY MA, AND DO THE CHORES,
AND SPEAK TO FOLKS POLITE,
MY BOTTLE SPREADS A RAINBOW-MIST, AND
FROM THE VAPOR FINE
TEN THOUSAND TROOPS FROM FAIRYLAND
COME RIDING IN A LINE.
I'VE SEEN THEM ON THEIR CHARGERS
RACE AROUND MY STUDY CHAIR,
THEY OPENED WIDE THE WINDOW AND
RODE FORTH UPON THE AIR.
THE ARMY WIDENED AS IT WENT, AND
INTO MYRIADS GREW,
OH, HOW THE LANCES SHIMMERED, HOW
THE SILVERY TRUMPETS BLEW!

THE MAGICAL VILLAGE

THE PATIENT WITCH.

A LADY CALLED THE PATIENT WITCH,
LIVED NEAR US LONG AGO.
OUR SERVANTS GAVE HER OFF AND ON
A BIT OF COIN OR SO,
TO TELL THEM WHAT THEIR DREAMS
    COULD MEAN,
AND IF THEIR LOVES WERE TRUE;
TO STUDY OUT THEIR PALMS AND SAY—
"A PALACE WAITS FOR YOU."
AND THEN SHE ALWAYS WAS POLITE,
AND SAID, "HOW DO YOU FARE?
I HOPE YOUR LITTLE GIRL IS WELL,"
WITH A MOST PLEASANT AIR.
SHE MUMBLED MUCH, WE KNEW NOT
    WHAT—
EACH AFTERNOON WOULD WAIT
BESIDE THE GUIDE-POST TO THE WEST
FOR SOME EXALTED FATE.
SHE LOOKED DOWN EVERY ROAD AS
    THOUGH
A STATELY COACH WAS DUE,
TO BEAR HER HOME TO SOMEWHERE
    ELSE,
TO FOLKS SHE REALLY KNEW.

"ONE EVENING," SAID A LITTLE BOY,
THE ONLY ONE ANIGH,
"SHE TOLD ME PRETTY STORIES, AND
SHE KISSED MY CURLS GOODBY,
AND TURNED INTO A SWAN AND SPREAD
HER WHITE WINGS BIG AND WIDE,
AND FLEW AND FLEW INTO THE SKY!
AND I CAME HOME AND CRIED."

EDEN IN WINTER.

SUPPOSED TO BE CHANTED TO SOME RUDE
INSTRUMENT AT A MODERN FIRE-
PLACE.

CHANT WE THE STORY NOW
THOUGH IN A HOUSE WE SLEEP.
THOUGH BY A HEARTH OF COALS
VIGIL TONIGHT WE KEEP.
CHANT WE THE STORY NOW,
OF THE VAGUE LOVE WE KNEW
WHEN I FROM OUT THE SEA
ROSE TO THE FEET OF YOU.
BIRD FROM THE CLIFFS YOU CAME
FLEW THROUGH THE SNOW TO ME,
FACING THE ICY BLAST
THERE BY THE ICY SEA.
HOW DID I REACH YOUR FEET?
WHY SHOULD I—AT THE END
HOLD OUT HALF FROZEN HANDS
DUMBLY TO YOU MY FRIEND?
NE'ER HAD I WOMAN SEEN,
NE'ER HAD I SEEN A FLAME.
THERE YOU PILED FAGOTS ON
HEAT ROSE—THE BLAST TO TAME.
THERE BY THE CAVE-DOOR DARK
COMFORTING ME YOU CRIED—
WAILED O'ER MY WOUNDED KNEE
WEPT FOR MY ROCK-TORN SIDE.
UP FROM THE SOUTH I TRAILED—
LEFT REGIONS FIERCE AND FAIR!
LEFT ALL THE JUNGLE-TREES
LEFT THE RED TIGER'S LAIR.

DREAM LED, I SCARCE KNEW WHY,
INTO YOUR NORTH I TROD—
NE'ER HAD I KNOWN THE SNOW,
OR THE FROST-BLASTED SOD.
OH HOW THE FLAKES CAME DOWN!
OH HOW THE FIRE BURNED HIGH!
STRANGE THING TO SEE HE WAS
THROUGH HIS DRY TWIGS WOULD FLY.
CREEP THERE AWHILE AND SLEEP—
THEN WAKE AND BARK FOR FIGHT—
BITING IF I TOO NEAR,
CAME TO HIS EYE SO BRIGHT.
THEN WITH A WILL YOU FED
WOOD TO HIS HUNGRY TONGUE.
THEN HE DID LEAP AND SING—
DANCING THE CLOUDS AMONG.
TURNING THE NIGHT TO NOON,
STINGING MY EYES WITH LIGHT,
MAKING THE SNOW RETREAT,
MAKING THE CAVE-HOUSE BRIGHT.
THERE WERE DRY FAGOTS PILED,
NUTS AND DRY LEAVES AND ROOTS,
STORES THERE OF FURS AND HIDES,
SWEET-BARKS AND GRAINS AND FRUITS.
THERE WRAPPED IN FUR WE LAY
HALF-BURNED, HALF-FROZEN STILL—
NE'ER WILL MY SOUL FORGET
ALL THE NIGHT'S BITTER CHILL.
WE HAD NOT LEARNED TO SPEAK
I WAS TO YOU A STRANGE
WOLFLING OR WOUNDED FAWN
LOST FROM HIS FOREST-RANGE.
THIRSTING FOR BLOODY MEAT
OUT AT THE DAWN WE WENT,
WEIGHED WITH OUR PREY AT EVE,
HOME-CAME WE ALL FORESPENT.
COMRADES AND HUNTERS TRIED
ERE WE WERE MAID AND MAN—
NOT TILL THE SPRING AWOKE
LAUGHTER AND SPEECH BEGAN
WHINING LIKE FOREST DOGS,
RUSTLING LIKE BUDDING TREES,
BUBBLING LIKE THAWING SPRINGS.
HUMMING LIKE LITTLE BEES,
CROONING LIKE MAYTIME TIDES,
CHATTERING PARROT WORDS,
CRYING THE PANTHER'S CRY,
CHIRPING LIKE MATING BIRDS—
THUS, THUS, WE LEARNED TO SPEAK,
WHO, 'MID THE SNOWS WERE DUMB,
NOR DID WE LEARN TO KISS
UNTIL THE SPRING HAD COME.

THE TOWER BUILDER.

IN AN IMPERIAL HOUR
WITH COUNTENANCE BENIGN,
VENUS THE HOLY CAME
AND LAID KIND HANDS IN MINE.
HANDS I CANNOT FORGET.
NEVER A WORD SHE SPOKE.
SHE GAVE HER FINGER-TIPS
AND MY DEAD SOUL AWOKE.
I LEARNED WHY STRONG MEN TOIL,
AND WHY BRIGHT CITIES RISE.
I HARDLY TOUCHED HER HAIR,
AND SCARCELY SAW HER EYES.

THOUGH SHE IS GONE I BUILD
BY HER STRONG HANDS ALL DAY.
I HAVE THE KEY TO LIFE
A POWER WORDS CANNOT SAY.

QUEEN MAB IN THE VILLAGE.

OH, ONCE I LOVED A FAIRY,
QUEEN MAB IT WAS. HER VOICE
WAS LIKE A LITTLE FOUNTAIN
THAT BIDS THE BIRDS REJOICE.
HER FACE WAS WISE AND SOLEMN,
HER HAIR WAS BROWN AND FINE.
HER DRESS WAS PANSY VELVET,
A BUTTERFLY DESIGN.
TO SEE HER HOVER ROUND ME
OR WALK THE HILLS OF AIR,
AWAKENED LOVE'S DEEP PULSES
AND BOYHOOD'S FIRST DESPAIR;
A PASSION LIKE A SWORD-BLADE
THAT PIERCED ME THROUGH AND
    THROUGH,
HER FINGERS HEALED THE SORROW
HER WHISPER WOULD RENEW.
WE SIGHED AND REIGNED AND FEASTED
WITHIN A HOLLOW TREE,
WE VOWED OUR LOVE WAS BOUNDLESS
ETERNAL AS THE SEA.
SHE BANISHED FROM HER KINGDOM
THE MORTAL BOY I GREW—
SO TALL AND CRUDE AND NOISY,
I KILLED GRASSHOPPERS TOO.
I THREW BIG ROCKS AT PIGEONS,
I PLUCKED AND TORE APART
THE WEEPING, WAILING DAISIES,
AND BROKE MY LADY'S HEART.
AT LENGTH I GREW TO MANHOOD,
I SCARCELY COULD BELIEVE,
I EVER LOVED THE LADY,
OR CAUSED HER COURT TO GRIEVE,
UNTIL A DREAM CAME TO ME
ONE BLEAK FIRST NIGHT OF SPRING
'ERE TIDES OF APPLE BLOSSOMS
ROLLED IN O'ER EVERYTHING,
WHILE RAIN AND SLEET AND SNOWBANKS
WERE STILL A VEXING MEN,
'ERE ROBIN AND HIS COMRADES
WERE NESTING ONCE AGAIN.
I SAW MAB'S BOOK OF JUDGMENT—
ITS CLASPS WERE IRON AND STONE,
ITS LEAVES WERE MAMMOTH IVORY,
ITS BOARDS WERE MAMMOTH BONE,—
HID IN HER SEASIDE MOUNTAINS,
FORGOTTEN OR UNKEPT,
BENEATH ITS MIGHTY COVERS
HER WRATH AGAINST ME SLEPT.
AND DEEPLY I REPENTED
OF BRASH AND BOYISH CRIME,
OF MURDER OF THINGS LOVELY
NOW AND IN OLDEN TIME.
I CURSED MY VAIN AMBITION,
MY WOULD-BE WORLDLY DAYS,
AND CRAVED THE PATHS OF WONDER,
OF DEWY DAWNS AND FAYS.
I CRIED, "OUR LOVE WAS BOUNDLESS
ETERNAL AS THE SEA,
OH, QUEEN, REVERSE THE SENTENCE,
COME BACK AND MASTER ME!"
THE BOOK WAS BY THE CLIFF-SIDE

UPON ITS EDGE UPRIGHT.
I LAID ME BY IT SOFTLY,
AND WEPT THROUGHOUT THE NIGHT.
AND THERE AT DAWN I SAW IT,
NO BOOK NOW BUT A DOOR,
UPON ITS PANELS WRITTEN
"JUDGMENT IS NO MORE."
THE BOLT FLEW BACK WITH THUNDER,
I SAW WITHIN THAT PLACE
A MERMAID WRAPPED IN SEAWEED
WITH MAB'S IMMORTAL FACE,
YET GROWN NOW TO A WOMAN,
A WOMAN TO THE KNEE.
SHE CRIED, SHE CLASPED ME FONDLY,
WE SOON WERE IN THE SEA.
AH, SHE WAS WISE AND SUBTLE,
AND GAY AND STRONG AND SLEEK,
WE CHAINED THE WICKED SWORD-FISH,
WE PLAYED AT HIDE AND SEEK.
WE FLOATED ON THE WATER,
WE HEARD THE DAWN-WIND SING,
I MADE FROM OCEAN-WONDERS
HER BRIDAL WREATH AND RING.
ALL MORTAL GIRLS WERE SHADOWS,
ALL EARTH-LIFE BUT A MIST,
WHEN DEEP BENEATH THE MAELSTROM,
THE MERMAID'S HEART I KISSED.
I WOKE BESIDE THE CHURCH-DOOR
OF OUR SMALL INLAND TOWN,
BOWING TO A MAIDEN
IN A PANSY-VELVET GOWN,
WHO HAD NOT HEARD OF FAIRIES,
YET SEEMED OF LOVE TO DREAM.
WE PLANNED AN EARTHLY COTTAGE
BESIDE AN EARTHLY STREAM.
OUR WEDDING LONG IS OVER,
WITH TOIL THE YEARS FILL UP,
YET IN THE EVENING SILENCE,
WE DRINK A DEEP-SEA CUP.
NOTHING THE FAY REMEMBERS,
YET WHEN SHE TURNS TO ME,
WE MEET BENEATH THE WHIRLPOOL,
WE SWIM THE GOLDEN SEA.

THE MASTER OF THE DANCE.

A MASTER DEEP-EYED
ERE HIS MANHOOD WAS RIPE,
HE SANG LIKE A THRUSH,
HE COULD PLAY ANY PIPE.
SO DULL IN THE SCHOOL
THAT HE SCARCELY COULD SPELL,
HE READ BUT A BIT,
AND HE FIGURED NOT WELL.
A BARE-FOOTED FOOL,
SHOD ONLY WITH GRACE;
LONG HAIR STREAMING DOWN
ROUND A WIND-HARDENED FACE;
HE SMILED LIKE A GIRL,
OR LIKE CLEAR WINTER SKIES,
A VIRGINAL LIGHT
MAKING STARS OF HIS EYES.
IN SWIFTNESS AND POISE,
A PROUD CHILD OF THE DEER,
A WHITE FAWN HE WAS,
YET A FAWN WITHOUT FEAR.
NO YOUTH THOUGHT HIM VAIN,
OR MADE MOCK OF HIS HAIR,
OR LAUGHED WHEN HIS WAYS

WERE MOST CURIOUSLY FAIR.
A MASTIFF AT FIGHT
HE COULD STRIKE TO THE EARTH
THE ENVIOUS ONE
WHO WOULD CHALLENGE HIS WORTH.
HOWEVER WE BOWED
TO THE SCHOOLMASTER MILD,
OUR SPIRITS WENT OUT
TO THE FAWN-FOOTED CHILD.
HIS BECKONING LED
OUR TROOP INTO THE BRUSH.
WE FOUND NOTHING THERE
BUT A WIND AND A HUSH.
HE SAT BY A STONE
AND HE LOOKED ON THE GROUND,
AS IF IN THE WEEDS
THERE WAS SOMETHING PROFOUND.
HIS PIPE SEEMED TO NEIGH,
THEN TO BLEAT LIKE A SHEEP,
THEN SOUND LIKE A STREAM
OR A WATERFALL DEEP.
IT WHISPERED STRANGE TALES,
HUMAN WORDS IT SPOKE NOT.
TOLD FAIR THINGS TO COME,
AND OUR MARVELOUS LOT
IF NOW WITH FAWN-STEPS
UNSHOD WE ADVANCED
TO THE MIDST OF THE GROVE
AND IN REVERENCE DANCED.
WE OBEYED AS HE PIPED
SOFT GRASS TO YOUNG FEET,
WAS A MEDICINE MIGHTY,
A REMEDY MEET.
OUR THIN BLOOD AWOKE,
IT GREW DIZZY AND WILD,
THOUGH SCARCELY A WORD
MOVED THE LIPS OF A CHILD.
OUR DANCE GAVE ALLEGIANCE,
IT SET US APART,
WE TRIPPED A STRANGE MEASURE,
UPLIFTED OF HEART.

II

WE THOUGHT TO BE PROUD
OF OUR FAWN EVERYWHERE.
WE COULD HARDLY SEE HOW
SIMPLE BOOKS WERE A CARE.
NO RULE OF THE SCHOOL
THIS STRANGE STUDENT COULD TAME.
HE WAS BANISHED ONE DAY,
WHILE WE QUIVERED WITH SHAME.
HE PIPED BACK OUR LOVE
ON A MOON-SILVERED NIGHT,
ENTICED US ONCE MORE
TO THE PLACE OF DELIGHT.
A GREETING HE SANG
AND IT MADE OUR BLOOD BEAT,
IT TRAMPED UPON CUSTOM
AND MOCKED AT DEFEAT.
HE BUILDED A FIRE
AND WE TRIPPED IN A RING,
THE EMBERS OUR BOOKS
AND THE FAWN OUR GOOD KING.
AND NOW WE APPROACHED
ALL THE MYSTERIES RARE
THAT SHADOWED HIS EYELIDS
AND BLEW THROUGH HIS HAIR.
THAT SPELL NOW WAS PEACE

THE DEEP STRENGTH OF THE TREES,
THE CHILDREN OF NATURE
WE CLAMBERED HER KNEES,
OUR BREATH AND OUR MOODS
WERE IN TUNE WITH HER OWN,
TREMENDOUS HER PRESENCE
ETERNAL HER THRONE.
THE OSTRACISED CHILD
OUR WHITE FOREHEADS KISSED,
OUR BODIES AND SOULS
BECAME LIGHTER THAN MIST.
SWEET DRESSES LIKE SNOW
OUR SMALL LADY-LOVES WORE,
LIKE MOONLIGHT THE THOUGHTS
THAT OUR BOSOMS UPBORE,
LIKE A LILY THE TOUCH
OF EACH COLD LITTLE HAND,
THE LOVES OF THE STARS
WE COULD NOW UNDERSTAND.
O QUIVERING AIR!
O THE CRYSTALLINE NIGHT!
O PAUSES OF AWE
AND THE FACES SWAN-WHITE!
O FERNS IN THE DUSK!
O FOREST-SHRINED HOUR!
O EARTH THAT SENT UP
THE VAST THRILL AND THE POWER.
TO LIFT US LIKE LEAVES
A DELIRIOUS WHIRL
THE MASTERFUL BOY
AND THE DELICATE GIRL!
WHAT CHILD THAT STRANGE NIGHT-TIME
CAN EVER FORGET?
HIS FEALTY DUE
AND HIS INFINITE DEBT
TO THE FOLLY DIVINE,
TO THE EXQUISITE RULE
OF THE PERILOUS MASTER
THE FAWN-FOOTED FOOL?

III

NOW SOLDIERS WE SEEM,
AND NIGHT BRINGS A NEW THING
A TERRIBLE IRE
AS OF THUNDER AWING.
A WARRIOR POWER,
THAT OLD CHIVALRY STIRRED,
WHEN KNIGHTS TOOK UP ARMS,
AS THE MAIDENS GAVE WORD.
THE END OF OUR WAR,
WILL BE WHITE-BANNERED DAYS,
WHEN THE TOWN LIKE A GREAT
BUDDING ROSE SHALL UPRAISE!
NEAR, NEARER THAT WAR,
AND THAT ECSTACY COMES,
WE HEAR THE TREES BEATING

INVISIBLE DRUMS.
THE FIELDS OF THE NIGHT
ARE STARLIGHTED ABOVE,
OUR GIRLS ARE WHITE TORCHES
OF CONQUEST AND LOVE.
NO NERVE WITHOUT WILL,
AND NO BREAST WITHOUT BREATH,
WE WHIRL WITH THE PLANETS
THAT NEVER KNOW DEATH!

THE DANDELION.

O DANDELION, RICH AND HAUGHTY,
KING OF VILLAGE FLOWERS!
EACH DAY IS CORONATION TIME,
YOU HAVE NO HUMBLE HOURS.
I LIKE TO SEE YOU BRING A TROOP
TO BEAT THE BLUE-GRASS SPEARS,
TO SCORN THE LAWN-MOWER THAT
WOULD BE
LIKE FATE'S TRIUMPHANT SHEARS.
YOUR YELLOW HEADS ARE CUT AWAY,
IT SEEMS YOUR REIGN IS O'ER.
BY NOON YOU RAISE A SEA OF STARS
MORE GOLDEN THAN BEFORE.

THE LAMP IN THE WINDOW.

I LIGHT MY HOMELY LAMP AGAIN TO-
NIGHT,
AND SAY"—PERHAPS A WANDERING ONE
GOES BY,
HURRIED PAST DOOR-WAYS WHERE THE
WATCH-DOGS GROWL—"
THE HEARTHS THE STRANGER DARES NOT
COME ANIGH.
WE SIT IN STOLID CIRCLE AT THE BOARD,
AND NEVER A SON OR DAUGHTER TELLS A
TALE.
THE FAITHFUL MOTHER FINDS NO CHEER
IN TOIL,
OUR ROSY INFANT'S CROW CAN NAUGHT
AVAIL.
THE COUNTRYSIDE GROWS DULL WITH
HOMES UNSTIRRED,
THE PREACHER PRATES IN LONG-FAMILIAR
WORDS.
THE NEIGHBORS COME, WITH WOODEN
EYES, TO TALK
OF WEEDS AND FENCES, BARNS AND
FLOCKS AND HERDS.
PERHAPS TONIGHT WITHIN THE SOAKING
RAIN
SOME STORM-BLOWN BOY MOVES ON THAT
WE SHOULD KEEP,
TO BRING US LAUGHTER ROUND OUR ROAR-
ING STOVE,
TO SHOW US WHY WE SOW AND WHY WE
REAP.
TONIGHT, PERCHANCE, A CONQUERING ONE
RETURNS,
MASTER OF WEARINESS AND FATE AND
PAIN
WITHIN HIS POCKET NOTE-BOOKS OF HIS
LORE,
WITHIN HIS SOUL GREAT PASSIONS HELD
IN REIN.
PERHAPS, TONIGHT SOME WILD MAN
PASSES BY,

BEARING WISE PARCHMENTS FROM OLD
CITIES GRIM,
OR, IT MAY BE, A BETTER LAMP THAN
MINE
MORE LIKE ALADDIN'S, NOT, LIKE THIS
ONE, DIM.
ALL IT WILL NEED, THE OIL AND WICK
AND FLAME,
AND SHELTERED ROOM TO KEEP THE WIND
AWAY
I CAN PROVIDE. AH, IF A LAMP HE
BRINGS,
IT SHALL BE TRIMMED AND BURNISHED
EVERY DAY!

THE HEARTH ETERNAL.

THERE DWELT A WIDOW LEANED AND DE-
VOUT,
BEHIND OUR HAMLET ON THE EASTERN
HILL.
THREE SONS SHE HAD, WHO WENT TO
FIND THE WORLD,
THEY PROMISED TO RETURN, BUT WAND-
ERED STILL.
THE CITIES USED THEM WELL, THEY WON
THEIR WAY,
RICH GIFTS THEY SENT, TO STILL THEIR
MOTHER'S SIGHS,
WORN OUT WITH HONORS, AND APART
FROM HER,
THEY DIED AS MANY A SELF-MADE EXILE
DIES.
THE MOTHER HAD A HEARTH THAT WOULD
NOT QUENCH,
THE DEATHLESS EMBERS FOUGHT THE
CREEPING GLOOM,
SHE SAID TO US WHO CAME WITH
WONDERING EYES—
"THIS IS A MAGIC FIRE, A MAGIC ROOM."
THE PINE BURNED OUT, BUT STILL THE
COALS GLOWED ON,
HER GRAVE GREW OLD BENEATH THE PEAR-
TREE SHADE,
AND YET HER CRUMBLING HOME EN-
SHRINED THE LIGHT,
THE NEIGHBORS PEERING IN WERE HALF-
AFRAID.
THEN STURDY BEGGARS, NEEDING FAGOTS
CAME,
ONE AT A TIME, AND STOLE THE WALLS,
AND FLOOR.
THEY LEFT A NAKED STONE, BUT HOW IT
BLAZED!
AND IN THE THUNDERSTORM IT FLARED
THE MORE.
AND NOW IT WAS THAT MEN WERE HEARD
TO SAY,
"THIS LIGHT SHOULD BE BELOVED BY ALL
THE TOWN."
AT LAST THEY MADE THE SLOPE A PLACE
OF PRAYER,
WHERE MARVELOUS THOUGHTS FROM GOD
CAME SWEEPING DOWN.
THEY LEFT THEIR CHURCHES CRUMBLING
IN THE SUN,
THEY MET ON THAT SOFT HILL, ONE
BROTHERHOOD;

ONE STRENGTH AND VALOR ONLY, ONE DE-
LIGHT,
ONE LAUGHING, BROODING GENIUS, GREAT
AND GOOD.
NOW MANY GREY-HAIRED PRODIGALS
COME HOME,
THE PLACE OUT-FLAMES THE CITIES OF
THE LAND,
AND TWICE-BORN BRAHMANS REACH US
FROM AFAR,
WITH SUBTLE EYES PREPARED TO UNDER-
STAND.
HIGHER AND HIGHER BURNS THE EASTERN
STEEP,
SHOWING THE ROADS THAT MARCH FROM
EVERYPLACE,
A STEADY BEACON O'ER THE WEARY
LEAGUES,
AT DEAD OF NIGHT IT LIGHTS THE TRAV-
ELLER'S FACE!
THUS HAS THE WIDOW CONQUERED HALF
THE EARTH,
SHE WHO INCREASED IN FAITH, THOUGH
ALL ALONE,
WHE KEPT HER EMPTY HOUSE A MAGIC
PLACE,
HAS MADE THE TOWN A HOLY ANGEL'S
THRONE.

THE BUSH OF BURNING SPICE.

FROM DUST CELESTIAL THAT A CLOUD LET
FALL,
A BUSH CAME UP, FULL FORTY YEARS UN-
SEEN,
THAT SCATTERED SMOKE AND EVER-BURN-
ING SPICE
ACROSS A FIELD OF THORNS AND BURDOCKS
MEAN.
AND THEN A CRIPPLED CHILD ON A SWEET
TIME,
OF HOLIDAY BEHELD IT DECK THE MORN.
HIS FRIEND, THE PASTOR, SAW ONE
BRANCH, AND SANG.
THE VILLAGE LAUGHED THE FLIGHTY PAIR
TO SCORN.
LATER THE TWO GROWN OLD AND STAID
DENIED,
THE SOLITARY INSIGHT OF THEIR YOUTH,
AND MOCKED THEIR CHILDREN, WHO WITH
LAUGHTER SANG,
"OUR EYES BEHOLD THE DEATHLESS BUSH
OF TRUTH."
"WHY DANCE, PRAY TELL," THE CRIPPLE
ASKED, "AND CHANT
AROUND A CINDER IN AN EMPTY LOT?"
"NO BURNING BUSH," THE PASTOR SAID,
"HAS BLOOMED
SINCE MOSES' DAY. NEW MIRACLES
COME NOT."
AND YET THOSE FRAGILE CHILDREN GREW
IN STRENGTH,
RADIANT AND ROYAL AS THE YEARS IN-
CREASED.
AT LAST THEY BROUGHT THEIR REVERENT
LOVERS THERE
TO BREATHE THE SMOKE AS THOUGH IT
WERE A FEAST.

FROM EVERY BRANCH FLEW OUT A RAIN-
BOW BIRD,
A DARLING SONGSTER WITH HIS PLUMES
AFLAME,
AND EVERY BIRD FLEW ROUND AND ROUND
A CHILD,
AND SANG OF GOD, AND CALLED THE CHILD
BY NAME.
THESE SWEETHEART'S NE'ER WERE FALSE.
EACH WOMAN WORE
WITHIN HER LOCKET SAFE, A FEATHER
BLUE,
THAT DROPPED TO HER FROM OUT THOSE
WHIRRING PLUMES,
A TALISMAN THAT KEPT HER LOVER TRUE.
AND YET IN AFTER TIME THOSE DAYS
GREW DIM,
AND LEST THEY BE FOREVER LEFT BEHIND
THEY WROTE THEM IN A BOOK IN NOBLE
WORDS,
SWEET HYMNS ABOUT A BUSH THEY
COULD NOT FIND!

THE WOMAN CALLED "BEAUTY" AND HER SEVEN DRAGONS.

A POEM FOR THOSE WHO DESIRE AN
ESTHETIC UTOPIA.

SHE BUILT TO THE HEIGHT OF HER
BREAST,
AN EARTH-WORK OF THISTLES AND SOD.
SHE LAVED HER SOFT ARMS IN THE
SPRING,
SHE SCATTERED THE FIRE WITH A ROD.
THE ROSE-PETAL CHILD BY HER SIDE,
CRIED OUT WITH A COUNTENANCE WHITE,
THE MOUND THEY HAD BUILDED AWOKE,
WITH EYES THAT WERE BLINKING AND
BRIGHT.
THE SEVEN STRANGE DRAGONS OF ART,
CAME FORTH LIKE GOLD PARCHMENTS UN-
ROLLED,
AND FAWNED ON THE SIBYL'S DOVE-HAND,
SUBMISSIVE AS SHEEP FROM THE FOLD.
YET SHIMMERING OPALS OF FIRE,
YET TITAN CHAMELEON—KINGS,
ALL HISSING IMPATIENTLY THERE,
UNSHEATHING THEIR TUSKS AND THEIR
STINGS.
SHE LAUGHED WHILE THEY FOAMED O'ER
THE FIELD,
AND BLASTED THE HEDGES WITH HEAT,
AND POUNDED THE BOULDERS TO DUST,
AND ATE THE RED FAGOTS LIKE MEAT.

II

GO FORTH, TEAR THIS IRON AGE DOWN,
"MY SONS," THUS THE WISE WOMAN
SPOKE,
"AND SET EVERY FANTASY FREE,
AND EVERY CRUSHED WORKER UNYOKE.
ESTABLISH THE SANDALWOOD AGE,
ESTABLISH THE WHITE AGE OF ART,
WHEN EARTH WILL STILL SIN AS OF OLD,
BUT SIN WITH A LOFTIER HEART.
WHEN CATIFFS AND BRAGGARTS WILL
SLAY,
BUT SLAY WITH A LOFTIER LUST,

WHEN LAUGHTER'S BRIGHT ROAD WILL BE
CLEAN,
AND TRAGEDY'S PATH MORE AUGUST.
WHEN YOUTH WILL CLIMB RECKLESSLY
STILL,
BUT CLIMB DRAGON-GREAT IN ITS PRIDE,
AND FULL-BLOODED, FURIOUS HOSTS,
WILL FLAUNT MY WHITE BANNER AND
RIDE
TO FIGHT AGAINST BALLOTS WITH TRUTH,
'GAINST MOBS, WITH THE CHISEL AND
PEN;
THE PRIZE OF MY SOLDIERS TO BE
FAIR CONTINENTS FITTED FOR MEN."

III

THE DRAGONS GAVE HEED TO THAT WORD,
LIKE FIELD-FLOWERS THEY BOWED TO HER
BREATH,
WHO MADE THEM AND ORDERED THEM
FORTH,
WITH POWERS OF CREATION AND DEATH.
THE CHILD SMOOTHED THEIR LEONINE
MANES.
FROM WIZARDRY HID IN THAT HAND,
THEY GREW AS THE THUNDER-CLOUDS
GROW,
ENCOMPASSING WATER AND LAND.
AND OH, HOW THEIR SERPENTINE SCALES
FLASHED, RATTLED AND CRASHED IN THE
AIR!
THEY CLIMBED WITH ALL-CONQUERING
COILS,
GOD'S CRYSTAL, IMPERIAL STAIR.
THEY ROARED THROUGH THE PATHWAYS
OF DAY,
SKY SWEEPING THEIR FOAM-FURROWS
FLEW,
THE SUN WAS AN ISLAND BESIEGED,
THEIR PENNONS TALL WAVES OF THE
BLUE.
BEHEMOTHS THEY WERE OF THAT TIDE,
OVERHEAD THAT MEN CALL THE HIGH
NOON,
THEIR CRIES IN BLOOD-STIRRING ACCORD,
LIKE TRUMPETS OF DOOMSDAY IN TUNE!

AND NOW THEY WERE GONE LIKE THE
WIND,
AND CLOUDLESS AND SILENT THE HOUR,
THE SIBYL WENT BACK TO THE TOWN,
AND HER SONS HURRIED FORTH IN HER
POWER.

THE SOUL OF A BUTTERFLY.

I STOOD ON THE WALL WITHOUT A DOOR,
WHERE THE HEAVEN OF HEAVENS BEGAN,
ON THE SHORE OF THE DRIED-UP DEEP OF
TIME,
AND DEATH AND HELL AND MAN.
BEHIND ME ROSE JERUSALEM,
WITH A HUNDRED WALLS ON HIGH,
TO THE ZENITH AND THE UPPER SOUTH,
TO THE HILLS ABOVE THE SKY.
I COULD NOT FACE THAT ROYAL TOWN,
WITH ITS SIDES OF SOARING LIGHT;
I STOOD ON THE LOWEST OUTER WALL
AND LOOKED TO THE NORTHERN NIGHT,
I CREPT TO THE EDGE OF THE ADAMANT,

AND PEERED DOWN THE AWFUL STEEP,
AND THE ANCIENT EARTH WAS A WILTING
FLOWER,
ON THE HEAVEN-LIT FIELDS OF THE DEEP.
I KNEW OLD WORMS CONSUMED HER FACE,
I KNEW ALL ELSE WAS FAIR,
I KNEW SHE WAS THE BLACKEST PLACE
WITHIN THE DEEPER AIR.
AT LAST A CLOUD FROM THE RIVER DEATH,
ROSE ROUND THAT TOMB OF MEN,
BUT A VOICE WITHIN ME CRIED TO ME,
"THE EARTH WILL LIVE AGAIN."
AND THE CLOUD OUTSPREAD AND HID
THE VOID,
AND FOUND NOT ANY REST,
TILL THE BOWL OF FATE WAS FILLED
WITH MIST,
TO THE LEVEL OF MY BREAST.
AND NOW ON THE NORTH HORIZON'S RIM
THE DEAD EARTH FLOATED, GRAY AND DIM,
IT SEEMED TO ALWAYS FLOAT TO ME,
AND THERE I WATCHED IT ENDLESSLY.

I SAW THAT DEAD EARTH BUD AND BLOOM,
AND FLASH WITH GOLD AND RED!
AND NOW IT LOOKED ME IN THE FACE,
A BUTTERFLY OF WONDROUS GRACE,
THE SOUL OF A GIANT BUTTERFLY
ARISEN FROM THE DEAD!

RELIGIOUS VERSES

HERE'S TO THE SPIRIT OF FIRE

HERE'S TO THE SPIRIT OF FIRE, WHEREVER
THE FLAME IS UNFURLED,
IN THE SUN, IT MAY BE, AS A TORCH, TO
LEAD ON AND ENLIGHTEN THE WORLD;
THAT MELTED THE GLACIAL STREAMS, IN
THE DAY THAT NO MEMORIES REACH,
THAT SHIMMERED IN AMBER AND SHELL
AND WEED ON THE EARLIEST BEACH;
THE GENIUS OF LOVE AND OF LIFE, THE
POWER THAT WILL EVER ABOUND,
THAT WAITS IN THE BONES OF THE DEAD,
WHO SLEEP TILL THE JUDGMENT
SHALL SOUND.
HERE'S TO THE SPIRIT OF FIRE, WHEN
CLOTHED IN SWIFT MUSIC IT COMES,
THE GLOW OF THE HARVESTING SONGS, THE
VOICE OF THE NATIONAL DRUMS;
THE WHIMSICAL, VARIOUS FIRE, IN THE
RHYMES AND IDEAS OF MEN,
BURIED IN BOOKS FOR AN AGE, EXPLODING
AND WRITHING AGAIN,
AND BLOWN A RED WIND ROUND THE
WORLD, CONSUMING THE LIES IN ITS
MIRTH,
THEN LOCKED IN DARK VOLUMES FOR
LONG, AND BURIED LIKE COAL IN THE
EARTH.
HERE'S TO THE COMFORTING FIRE IN THE
JOYS OF THE BLIND AND THE MEEK,
IN THE CUSTOMS OF LETTERLESS LANDS,
IN THE THOUGHTS OF THE STUPID
AND WEAK.
IN THE WEARIEST LEGENDS THEY TELL, IN
THEIR CRUELEST COLDEST BELIEF,

IN THE PROVERBS OF COUNTER OR TILL, IN
    THE ARTS OF THE PRIEST OR THE
    THIEF.
HERE'S TO THE SPIRIT OF FIRE, THAT
    NEVER THE OCEAN CAN DROWN,
THAT GLOWS IN THE PHOSPHORENT WAVE,
    AND GLEAMS IN THE SEA-ROSES
    CROWN;
THAT SLEEPS IN THE SUNBEAM AND MIST,
    THAT CREEPS AS THE WISE CAN BUT
    KNOW,
A WONDER, AN INCENSE, A WHIM, A PER-
    FUME, A FEAR AND A GLOW,
ENSNARING THE STARS WITH A SPELL,
    AND HOLDING THE EARTH IN A NET,
YEA, FILLING THE NATIONS WITH PRAYER,
    WHEREVER MAN'S PATHWAY IS SET.

LOOK YOU, I'LL GO PRAY.

LOOK YOU, I'LL GO PRAY,
MY SHAME IS CRYING,
MY SOUL IS GREY AND FAINT,
MY FAITH IS DYING.
LOOK YOU, I'LL GO PRAY—
"SWEET MARY, MAKE ME CLEAN,
THOU RAINSTORM OF THE SOUL,
THOU WINE FROM WORLD'S UNSEEN."

THE MISSIONARY MISGIVING.

(WILL THE WORLD BE BUT NOMINALLY
        CHRISTIAN?)

I SEE ANOTHER LUTHER
BRING WRATH TO INDIA'S EYES.
I SEE AN INQUISITION
BY CHINA'S CHURCHES RISE.
I SEE ANOTHER CROMWELL
SET FIRE TO GRIM JAPAN,
LONG IS THE ROAD AND DREADFUL,
WHEREBY CHRIST CONQUERS MAN.
OR, IF OUR CREEDS SHALL CRUMBLE?
WHAT IF THE AGES SEE,
A JESUS LIKE TO BUDDHA,
UNDER THE BOHDI TREE?
A CHRIST TOO LIKE CONFUCIUS,
WITH SILKEN ROBE AND FAN?
YET ARE THE YEARS TRIUMPHANT
IF CHRIST SHALL CONQUER MAN.

FOR CHRIST HAS COME IN GLORY,
WHEN MEN ARE BROTHERS HERE,
WHEN SWORDS ARE TURNED TO PLOUGH-
    SHARES,
AND PEACE HAS VANQUISHED FEAR.
WHATEVER TOMB ENFOLDS HIM,
HOWEVER STRANGE HIS PLAN,
THE EARTH SHALL BE HIS THRONE-ROOM,
OUR CHRIST SHALL CONQUER MAN!

FOREIGN MISSIONS IN BATTLE
ARRAY.

AN ENDLESS LINE OF SPLENDOR,
THESE TROOPS WITH HEAVEN FOR HOME,
WITH CREEDS THEY GO FROM SCOTLAND,
WITH INCENSE GO FROM ROME.
THESE, IN THE NAME OF JESUS,
AGAINST THE DARK GODS STAND,
THEY GIRD THE EARTH WITH VALOR,
THEY HEED THEIR KING'S COMMAND.

ONWARD THE LINE ADVANCES,
SHAKING THE HILLS WITH POWER,
SLAYING THE HIDDEN DEMONS,
THE LIONS THAT DEVOUR.
NO BLOODSHED IN THE WRESTLING,—
BUT SOULS NEW-BORN ARISE—
THE NATIONS GROWING KINDER,
THE CHILD-HEARTS GROWING WISE.

WHAT IS THE FINAL ENDING?
THE ISSUE, CAN WE KNOW?
WILL CHRIST OUTLIVE MOHAMMED?
WILL KALI'S ALTAR GO?
THIS IS OUR FAITH TREMENDOUS,—
OUR WILD HOPE, WHO SHALL SCORN,—
THAT IN THE NAME OF JESUS
THE WORLD SHALL BE REBORN!

GALAHAD, KNIGHT WHO PERISHED.
A POEM DEDICATED TO ALL CRUSADERS
    AGAINST THE INTERNATIONAL AND
    INTERSTATE TRAFFIC IN
        YOUNG GIRLS.

GALAHAD * * * SOLDIER THAT PER-
    ISHED * * * AGES AGO,
OUR HEARTS ARE BREAKING WITH SHAME,
    OUR TEARS OVERFLOW.
GALAHAD * * * KNIGHT WHO PER-
    ISHED * * * AWAKEN AGAIN,
TEACH US TO FIGHT FOR IMMACULATE
    WAYS AMONG MEN.
SOLDIERS FANTASTIC, WE PRAY TO THE
    STAR OF THE SEA,
WE PRAY TO THE MOTHER OF GOD THAT
    WHITE SLAVES MAY BE FREE.
ROSE-CROWNED LADY FROM HEAVEN, GIVE
    US THY GRACE,
HELP US THE DESPERATE, DESPERATE BAT-
    TLE TO FACE
TILL THE LEER OF THE TRADER IS SEEN
    NEVERMORE IN THE LAND,
TILL WE BRING EVERY MAID OF THE AGE
    TO ONE SHELTERING HAND.
AH, THEY ARE PRICELESS, THE PALE AND
    THE IVORY AND RED!
BREATHLESS WE GAZE ON THE CURLS OF
    EACH GLORIOUS HEAD!
ARM THEM WITH STRENGTH MEDIEVAL,
    THY MARVELOUS DOWER,
BLAST NOW THEIR TEMPTERS, SHELTER
    THEIR STEPS WITH THY POWER.
LEAVE NOT LIFE'S FAIREST TO PERISH—
    STRANGERS TO THEE,
LET NOT THE WEAKEST BE SHIPWRECKED,
    OH, STAR OF THE SEA!

THE PERILOUS ROAD.
A POEM FOR SPIRITUALISTS.

"HERMIT," THE YOUTH SAID, "TEACH MY
    HEART THE WAYS
OF HEAVEN'S FREE DAYS.
AND ARE THEIR PLEASURES VARIOUS,
    FRAGILE, FLEET
WHERE BRIGHT SOULS MEET?
FATHER IN GOD, FOR I HAVE FASTED LONG,
    TEACH A WILD SONG.
TEACH ME, THE WHILE I KNEEL, A CURI-
    OUS PRAYER
TO RULE THE AIR.

SHOW ME THE SECRET DOOR THAT OPENS
    WIDE
WHERE CHARIOTS RIDE.
CHARIOTS THAT COME TO WHIRL YOU TO
    THE SKY,
WHEN EVE IS NIGH,
CHARIOTS THAT BEAR YOU BACK TO TIME
    AND SPACE,
AND THIS GRIM PLACE."
"NAY," SAID THE PALSIED MAN, "I KEEP
    THE SPELL
OF HEAVEN, OF HELL.
NAY, THOUGH YOU KNEEL, GOOD YOUTH,
    I WILL NOT SHOW
WHAT HERMITS KNOW.
SELDOM I DARE TO OPEN WIDE MINE EYES,
BY THAT PATH LIES
TERROR, AND ROSE-BRIARS FIERCE WILL
    PIERCE AND SEAR,
THIS OLD FRAME HERE.
HE WHO WOULD SPEAK TO STRANGERS IN
    THE NIGHT
GOING BY, IN WHITE:
HE WHO WOULD SPEAK TO CHRIST IN
    FUNERAL ROOMS
AND BY NEW TOMBS:
WHO WOULD TOUCH THE HOT-WINGED,
    TALL IMMORTAL MEN,
AND RETURN AGAIN:
MUST SCORN HIS DAILY LIFE AND NATURAL
    FRIENDS,
SUCH FRIENDSHIP ENDS.
HE MUST LEAVE HIS SWEETHEART WEEP-
    ING IN THE LANE,
TO FORESTALL HER PAIN
WHEN HE WAKES ONCE MORE, HER FIND-
    ING HIM SO COLD
TO THEIR LOVE OF OLD.
A HEAVEN OF HEAVENS IS NOT ALWAYS
    WORTH
A SURRENDERED EARTH.
ONE BLAST OF THAT PERILOUS AIR DRIES
    UP THE HEART,
YEA, IT SETS APART
FROM ALL THINGS HERE THE SEER, HALF
    MAD, ALONE,
LIKE A LEAF, A STONE."

HEART OF GOD.

A PRAYER IN THE JUNGLES OF HEAVEN.

O GREAT HEART OF GOD,
ONCE VAGUE AND LOST TO ME,
WHY DO I THROB WITH YOUR THROB TO-
    NIGHT,
IN THIS LAND, ETERNITY?
O LITTLE HEART OF GOD,
SWEET INTRUDING STRANGER,
YOU ARE LAUGHING IN MY HUMAN
    BREAST,
A CHRIST-CHILD IN A MANGER.
HEART, DEAR HEART OF GOD,
BESIDE YOU NOW I KNEEL,
STRONG HEART OF FAITH. O HEART NOT
    MINE,
WHERE GOD HAS SET HIS SEAL.
WILD THUNDERING HEART OF GOD
OUT OF MY DOUBT I COME,

AND MY FOOLISH FEET WITH PROPHETS'
    FEET,
MARCH WITH THE PROPHETS' DRUM.

IN MEMORY OF A CHILD.

I

THE ANGELS GUIDE HIM NOW,
AND WATCH HIS CURLY HEAD,
AND LEAD HIM IN THEIR GAMES,
THE LITTLE BOY WE LED.

II

HE CANNOT COME TO HARM,
HE KNOWS MORE THAN WE KNOW,
HIS LIGHT IS BRIGHTER FAR
THAN DAYTIME HERE BELOW.

III

HIS PATH LEADS ON AND ON,
THROUGH PLEASANT LAWNS AND FLOWERS,
HIS BROWN EYES OPEN WIDE
AT GRASS MORE GREEN THAN OURS.

IV

WITH PLAYMATES LIKE HIMSELF,
THE SHINING BOY WILL SING.
EXPLORING WONDROUS WOODS,
SWEET WITH ETERNAL SPRING.

V

YET, HE IS LOST TO US,
FAR IS HIS PATH OF GOLD,
FAR DOES THE CITY SEEM,
LONELY OUR HEARTS AND OLD.

RHYMES OF THE DAY AND HOUR

IN PRAISE OF SONGS THAT DIE.

AFTER HAVING READ A GREAT DEAL OF
GOOD CURRENT POETRY IN THE MAGAZINES
AND NEWSPAPERS.

AH, THEY ARE PASSING, PASSING BY,
WONDERFUL SONGS, BUT BORN TO DIE!
CRIES FROM THE INFINITE HUMAN SEAS,
WAVES THRICE-WINGED WITH HARMONIES.
HERE I STAND ON A PIER IN THE FOAM
SEEING THE SONGS TO THE BEACH GO
    HOME
DYING IN SAND WHILE THE TIDE FLOWS
    BACK,
AS IT FLOWED OF OLD IN ITS FATED TRACK.
OH HURRYING TIDE THAT WILL NOT HEAR
YOUR OWN FOAM-CHILDREN DYING NEAR:
IS THERE NO REFUGE-HOUSE OF SONG,
NO HOME, NO HAVEN WHERE SONGS BE-
    LONG?
OH PRECIOUS HYMNS THAT COME AND GO!
YOU PERISH, AND I LOVE YOU SO!

FORMULA FOR A UTOPIA.

LET EVERY CHILD BE BORN OF PASSIONATE
    LOVE,
CRADLED IN TENDERNESS AND SACRED JOY:
GAY LITTLE MAIDENS WITH THE HEARTS
    OF NUNS—
LET GALAHAD BE BORN IN EVERY BOY.

241

THE PERFECT MARRIAGE.

I.

I HATE THIS YOKE; FOR THE WORLD'S
SAKE HERE PUT IT ON:
KNOWING 'TWILL WEIGH AS MUCH ON
YOU TILL LIFE IS GONE.
KNOWING YOU LOVE YOUR FREEDOM DEAR,
AS I LOVE MINE—
KNOWING THAT LOVE UNCHAINED HAS
BEEN OUR LIFE'S GREAT WINE:
OUR ONE GREAT WINE, (YET SPENT TOO
SOON, AND SERVING NONE;
OF THE TWO CUPS FREE LOVE AT LAST THE
DEADLY ONE.)

II.

WE GRANT OUR MEETINGS WILL BE TAME,
NOT HONEY-SWEET,
NO LONGER TURNING TO THE TRYST WITH
FLYING FEET.
WE KNOW THE TOIL THAT NOW MUST
COME WILL SPOIL THE BLOOM
AND TENDERNESS OF PASSION'S TOUCH,
AND IN IT'S ROOM
WILL COME TAME HABIT, DEADLY CALM,
SORROW AND GLOOM.
OH HOW THE BATTLE SCARS THE BEST WHO
ENTER LIFE!
EACH SOLDIER COMES OUT BLIND OR LAME
FROM THE BLACK STRIFE.
MAD OR DISEASED OR DAMNED OF SOUL
THE BEST MAY COME—
IT MATTERS NOT HOW MERRILY NOW
ROLLS THE DRUM,
THE FIFE SHRILLS HIGH, THE HORN
SINGS LOUD, TILL NO STEPS LAG—
AND ALL ADORE THAT SILKEN FLAME,
DESIRE'S GREAT FLAG.

III.

WE WILL BUILD STRONG OUR TINY FORT,
STRONG AS WE CAN—
HOLDING ONE INNER ROOM BEYOND THE
SWORD OF MAN.
LOVE IS TOO WIDE, IT SEEMS TODAY, TO
HIDE IT THERE,
IT SEEMS TO FLOOD THE FIELDS OF CORN,
AND GILD THE AIR—
IT SEEMS TO BREATHE FROM EVERY BROOK,
FROM FLOWERS TO SIGH—
IT SEEMS A CATARACT POURED DOWN
FROM THE GREAT SKY;
IT SEEMS A TENDERNESS SO VAST NO BUSH
BUT SHOWS

ITS HAUNTING AND TRANSFIGURING LIGHT
WHERE WONDER GLOWS.
IT WRAPS US IN A SILKEN SNARE BY
SHADOWY STREAMS.
AND WILDERING SWEET AND STUNG WITH
JOY YOUR WHITE SOUL SEEMS
A FLAME, A FLAME, CONQUERING DAY,
CONQUERING NIGHT,
BROUGHT FROM OUR GOD, A HOLY THING,
A MAD DELIGHT.
BUT LOVE, WHEN ALL THINGS BEAT IT
DOWN, LEAVES THE WIDE AIR,
THE HEAVENS ARE GREY, AND MEN TURN
WOLVES, LEAN WITH DESPAIR.
AH, WHEN WE NEED LOVE MOST, AND
WEEP, WHEN ALL IS DARK,
LOVE IS A PINCH OF ASHES GREY, WITH
ONE LIVE SPARK—
YET ON THE HOPE TO KEEP ALIVE THAT
TREASURE STRANGE
HANGS ALL EARTH'S STRUGGLE, STRIFE
AND SCORN, AND DESPERATE CHANGE.

IV.

LOVE? * * * WE WILL SCARCELY LOVE
OUR BABES, FULL, MANY A TIME—
KNOWING THEIR SOULS AND OURS TOO
WELL, AND ALL OUR GRIME—
AND THERE BESIDE OUR HOLY HEARTH
WE'LL HIDE OUR EYES—
LEST WE SHOULD FLASH WHAT SEEMS
DISDAIN WITHOUT DISGUISE.
YET THERE SHALL BE NO WAVERING THERE
IN THAT DEEP TRIAL—
AND NO FALSE FIRE OR STRANGER HAND OR
TRAITOR VILE—
WE'LL FIGHT THE GLOOM AND FIGHT THE
WORLD WITH STRONG SWORD-PLAY,
ENTRENCHED WITHIN OUR BLOCK-HOUSE
SMALL, EVER AT BAY—
AS FELLOW-WARRIORS, UNDERPAID, WOUND-
ED AND WILD,
TRUE TO THEIR BATTERED FLAG, THEIR
FAITH STILL UNDEFILED!

V.

WE WILL DO WELL. WE'LL SAVE THROUGH
LIFE LOVE'S SPARK, LOVE'S GEM,
WE'LL GUARD NO MAN-MADE HEAP OF
COINS OR DIADEM—
BUT CLASP WORN HANDS, AND VOW GREAT
VOWS TO GOD ABOVE,
KEEPING UNQUENCHED THROUGH STORM
AND FEAR, ONE SPARK OF LOVE!

THE LEADEN EYED.

LET NOT YOUNG SOULS BE SMOTHERED OUT
  BEFORE
THEY DO QUAINT DEEDS AND FULLY
  FLAUNT THEIR PRIDE.
IT IS THE WORLD'S ONE CRIME ITS BABES
  GROW DULL,
ITS POOR ARE OX-LIKE, LIMP AND LEADEN
  EYED.
NOT THAT THEY STARVE, BUT STARVE SO
  DREAMLESSLY,
NOT THAT THEY SOW, BUT THAT THEY
  SELDOM REAP,
NOT THAT THEY SERVE, BUT HAVE NO GODS
  TO SERVE,
NOT THAT THEY DIE, BUT THAT THEY DIE
  LIKE SHEEP.

THE FOLLOWING VERSES WERE WRITTEN
ON THE EVENING OF MARCH THE FIRST,
NINETEEN HUNDRED AND ELEVEN, AND
PRINTED NEXT MORNING IN THE ILLINOIS
STATE REGISTER.

THEY CELEBRATE THE ARRIVAL OF THE
NEWS THAT THE UNITED STATE SENATE
HAD DECLARED THE ELECTION OF WILLIAM
LORIMER GOOD AND VALID, BY A VOTE OF
FORTY-SIX TO FORTY.

TO THE UNITED STATES SENATE.

REVELATION 16: VERSES 16 THROUGH 19.

AND MUST THE SENATOR FROM ILLINOIS
BE THIS SQUAT THING, WITH BLINKING,
  HALF-CLOSED EYES?
THIS BRAZEN GUTTER IDOL, REARED TO
  POWER
UPON A LEERING PYRAMID OF LIES?
AND MUST THE SENATOR FROM ILLINOIS
BE THE WORLD'S PROVERB OF SUCCESSFUL
  SHAME,
DAZZLING ALL STATE HOUSE FLIES THAT
  STEAL AND STEAL,
WHO, WHEN THE SAD STATE SPARES
  THEM, COUNT IT FAME?
IF ONCE OR TWICE WITHIN HIS NEW WON
  HALL
HIS VOTE HAD COUNTED FOR THE BROKEN
  MEN;
IF IN HIS EARLY DAYS HE WROUGHT
  SOME GOOD——
WE MIGHT A GREAT SOUL'S SINS FORGIVE
  HIM THEN.
BUT MUST THE SENATOR FROM ILLINOIS
BE VINDICATED BY FAT KINGS OF GOLD?
AND MUST HE BE BELAUDED BY THE
  SMIRCHED,
THE SLEEK, UNCANNY CHIEFS IN LIES
  GROWN OLD?
BE WARNED, OH, WANTON ONES, WHO
  SHIELDED HIM——
BLACK WRATH AWAITS. YOU ALL SHALL
  EAT THE DUST.
YOU DARE NOT SAY: "TOMORROW WILL
  BRING PEACE;
LET US MAKE MERRY, AND GO FORTH IN
  LUST."
WHAT WILL YOU TRADING FROGS DO ON A
  DAY

WHEN ARMAGEDDON THUNDERS THROUGH
  THE LAND;
WHEN EACH SAD PATRIOT RISES, MAD
  WITH SHAME,
HIS BALLOT OR HIS MUSKET IN HIS HAND?
IN THE DISTRACTED STATES FROM WHICH
  YOU CAME
THE DAY IS BIG WITH WAR HOPES FIERCE
  AND STRANGE;
OUR IRON CHICAGOS AND OUR GRIMY
  MINES
RUMBLE WITH HATE AND LOVE AND SOL
  EMN CHANGE.
TOO MANY WEARY MEN SHED HONEST
  TEARS,
GROUND BY MACHINES THAT GIVE THE
  SENATE EASE.
TOO MANY LITTLE BABES WITH BLEEDING
  HANDS
HAVE HEAPED THE FRUITS OF EMPIRE ON
  YOUR KNEES.
AND SWINE WITHIN THE SENATE IN THIS
  DAY,
WHEN ALL THE SMOTHERING BY-STREETS
  WEEP AND WAIL;
WHEN WISDOM BREAKS THE HEARTS OF
  HER BEST SONS;
WHEN KINGLY MEN, VOTING FOR TRUTH,
  MAY FAIL:——
THESE ARE A PORTENT AND A CALL TO
  ARMS.
OUR PROTEST TURNS INTO A BATTLE CRY:
"OUR SHAME MUST END, OUR STATES BE
  FREE AND CLEAN;
AND IN THIS WAR WE CHOOSE TO LIVE
  AND DIE."

DREAMS IN THE SLUM.

SOME MEN, NOT BLIND, STILL THINK AMID
  THE FILTH.
SOME SCHOLARS SEE VAST CITIES LIKE
  THE SUN:
BRIGHT HIVES OF POWER, OF JUSTICE AND
  OF LOVE,
IN BRAINS LIKE THESE OUR ZION HAS
  BEGUN.
WHAT WILL YOU DO TO MAKE THEIR
  THOUGHT COME TRUE?
OR WILL YOU TREAD THEIR PEARLS INTO
  THE EARTH?
FRIENDS, WHEN SUCH VOICES RISE DESPITE
  THE TIME,
WHAT ARE YOUR SHABBY, RICH MAN'S
  TEMPLES WORTH?

THE EAGLE THAT IS FORGOTTEN.

(JOHN P. ALTGELD. BORN DEC. 30, 1847;
  DIED MARCH 12, 1902.)

SLEEP SOFTLY * * * EAGLE FORGOTTEN
  * * * UNDER THE STONE,
TIME HAS ITS WAY WITH YOU THERE, AND
  THE CLAY HAS ITS OWN.
"WE HAVE BURIED HIM NOW," THOUGHT
  YOUR FOES, AND IN SECRET REJOICED.
THEY MADE A BRAVE SHOW OF THEIR
  MOURNING, THEIR HATRED UNVOICED.

243

THEY HAD SNARLED AT YOU, BARKED AT
YOU, FOAMED AT YOU DAY AFTER DAY,
NOW YOU WERE ENDED. THEY PRAISED
YOU, * * * AND LAID YOU AWAY.
THE OTHERS THAT MOURNED YOU IN
SILENCE AND TERROR AND TRUTH.
THE WIDOW BEREFT OF HER CRUST, AND
THE BOY WITHOUT YOUTH,
THE MOCKED AND THE SCORNED AND THE
WOUNDED, THE LAME AND THE POOR
THAT SHOULD HAVE REMEMBERED FOR-
EVER, * * * REMEMBER NO MORE.
WHERE ARE THOSE LOVERS OF YOURS, ON
WHAT NAME DO THEY CALL
THE LOST, THAT IN ARMIES WEPT OVER
YOUR FUNERAL PALL?
THEY CALL ON THE NAMES OF A HUNDRED
HIGH-VALIANT ONES,
A HUNDRED WHITE EAGLES HAVE RISEN
THE SONS OF YOUR SONS,
THE ZEAL IN THEIR WINGS IS A ZEAL THAT
YOUR DREAMING BEGAN
THE VALOR THAT WORE OUT YOUR SOUL IN
THE SERVICE OF MAN.
SLEEP SOFTLY, * * * EAGLE FORGOTTEN,
* * * UNDER THE STONE,
TIME HAS ITS WAY WITH YOU THERE
AND THE CLAY HAS ITS OWN.
SLEEP ON, O BRAVE HEARTED, O WISE MAN,
THAT KINDLED THE FLAME—
TO LIVE IN MANKIND IS FAR MORE THAN
TO LIVE IN A NAME,
TO LIVE IN MANKIND, FAR FAR MORE * *
THAN TO LIVE IN A NAME.

TO THOSE THAT WOULD MEND
THESE TIMES.

GO PLANT THE ARTS THAT WOO THE
WEARIEST,
BOLD ARTS THAT SIMPLE WORKMEN UN-
DERSAND,
THAT MAKE NO POOR MEN AND KEEP ALL
MEN RICH,
AND THRONE OUR LADY BEAUTY IN THE
LAND!

TO THOSE THAT WOULD HELP THE
FALLEN.

GO PLANT THE CRAFTS THAT GIVE A DEEP
DELIGHT
TO ALL WHO MAKE, TO ALL WHO USE
AND SEE:—
NEW CRAFTS WHERE ROUGHEST MEN CAN
HINT AT THE THOUGHT
AND WRITE LIFE'S LYRIC IN A HAND SET
FREE:
THE DEATHLESS TOUCH OF AGES WORKED
ANEW
UPON THE DOOR OF EVERY TINIEST ROOM:
THE JOY OF LIVING PAINTED ON THE
WALLS,
AND DAZZLING FABRICS WROUGHT ON ART'S
HOME-LOOM.
DECKING THE PARKS: VAIR, VELVET, SILK
AND GOLD:

OLD PAGEANTS MARCHING THAT WERE
LONG-TIME DEAD:
INNOCENT GAMBOLS, HARP AND SONG
AFOOT:—
TO PRAISE THE DAY WHEN ART AND FREE-
DOM WED!

THE TRAP.

SHE WAS TAUGHT DESIRE IN THE STREET
NOT AT THE ANGEL'S FEET.
BY THE GOOD NO WORD WAS SAID
OF THE WORTH OF THE BRIDAL BED.
THE SECRET WAS LEARNED FROM THE VILE
NOT FROM HER MOTHER'S SMILE.
HOME SPOKE NOT. AND THE GIRL
WAS CAUGHT IN THE PUBLIC WHIRL.
DO YOU SAY "SHE GAVE CONSENT:
LIFE DRUNK, SHE WAS CONTENT
WITH BEASTS THAT HER FIRE COULD
PLEASE?"
BUT SHE DID NOT CHOOSE DISEASE
OF MIND AND NERVES AND BREATH.
SHE WAS TRAPPED TO A SLOW, FOUL
DEATH.
THE DOOR WAS WATCHED SO WELL,
THAT THE STEEP DARK STAIR TO HELL
WAS THE ONLY ESCAPING WAY * * *
"SHE GAVE CONSENT," YOU SAY?
SOME THINK SHE WAS MEEK AND GOOD
ONLY LOST IN THE WOOD
OF YOUTH, AND DECEIVED IN MAN
WHEN THE HUNGER OF SEX BEGAN
THAT TIES THE HUSBAND AND WIFE
TO THE END IN A STRONG FOND LIFE.
HER CAPTOR. BY CHANCE WAS ONE
OF THOSE WHOSE PASSION WAS DONE,
A COLD FIERCE WORM OF THE SEA
ENSLAVING FOR YOU AND ME.
THE WAGES THE POOR MUST TAKE
HAVE FORCED THEM TO SERVE THIS SNAKE.
YEA, HALF-PAID GIRLS MUST GO
FOR BREAD TO HIS PIT BELOW.
WHAT HANGMAN SHALL WAIT HIS HOST
OF BUTCHERS FROM COAST TO COAST,
NEW YORK TO THE GOLDEN GATE—
THE MERGER OF DEATH AND FATE,
LUST-KINGS WITH A CAREFUL PLAN
CLEAN-CUT, AMERICAN?
OH MOTHERS WHO FAILED TO TELL
THE MAZES OF HEAVEN AND HELL,
WHO FAILED TO ADVISE, IMPLORE
YOUR DAUGHTER AT LOVE'S STRANGE DOOR
WHAT WILL YOU DO THIS DAY?
YOUR DEAR ONES ARE HIDDEN AWAY,
AS GOOD AS CHAINED TO THE BED
HID LIKE THE MAD, OR THE DEAD:—
THE GLORIES OF ENDLESS YEARS
DROWNED IN THEIR HARLOT-TEARS:
THE CHILDREN THEY HOPED TO BEAR
GRANDCHILDREN STRONG AND FAIR
THE LIFE FOR AGES TO BE
CUT OFF LIKE A BLASTED TREE.
MURDERED IN FILTH IN A DAY,
SOMEHOW, BY THE MERCHANT GAY!
IN LIBERTY'S NAME WE CRY
FOR THESE WOMEN ABOUT TO DIE.

WHAT SHALL BE SAID OF A STATE
WHERE TRAPS FOR THE WHITE BRIDES
    WAIT?
OF SELLERS OF DRINK WHO PLAY
THE GAME FOR THE EXTRA PAY?
OF STATESMEN IN LEAGUE WITH ALL
WHO HOPE FOR THE GIRL-CHILD'S FALL?
OF BANKS WHERE HELL'S MONEY IS PAID
AND PHARISEES ALL AFRAID
OF PANDARS THAT HELP THEM SIN?
WHEN WILL OUR WRATH BEGIN?

TO REFORMERS IN DESPAIR.

'TIS NOT TOO LATE TO BUILD OUR YOUNG
    LAND RIGHT,
CLEANER THAN HOLLAND, COURTLIER THAN
    JAPAN,
DEVOUT LIKE EARLY ROME, WITH HEARTHS
    LIKE HERS,
HEARTHS THAT WILL RECREATE THE BREED
    CALLED MAN.

POEMS ON THE FAR DISTANT FUTURE

THE LEGISLATURE.

OUT OF THE HEART OF AGES COMES THE
    LAW,
THE SONS WILL HONOR WHAT THE SIRES
    HAVE LEFT:
THEIR PROVERB IS THE FATHERS' CARE-
    LESS WIT,
THEIR HONESTY THE FATHERS' CARELESS
    THEFT.
WHAT IS OUR FREEDOM BUT A CHANCE
    TO GIVE
POSTERITY A NOBLE HOUSE FOR PLAY?
AND WILL OUR CHECKED AND BALANCED
    LAWS BE CHAINS
TO HANG OUR CHILDREN IN AN EVIL DAY?
WE SAY WE WANT THE NATION TO BE
    FREE,
YET THERE'S A CLANK IN EVERY LAW
    WE WRITE.
WHY SHOULD WE WORK AT SUCH ILL-
    OMENED STEEL?
TODAY THE FORGE IS LOUD, THE METAL
    WHITE.
TODAY MAD BLOWS COME THICK AND FAST.
    THE STEEL
YIELDS WELL, THAT SOON WILL COOL FOR-
    EVERMORE.
WHAT HAVE OUR WILD BLOWS WROUGHT?
    WHAT GRACELESS MOULD
WHERE MEN WILL POUR THEIR BLOOD
    FOREVERMORE?

THE PILGRIMS FROM ASIA.
(IN THE DISTANT FUTURE.)

I HAVE WATCHED MULTITUDES OF SCHOL-
    ARS COME
TO HAUNT YOUR FOOT-STEPS, LINCOLN, IN
    OUR TOWN;
EACH PILGRIM PACING FROM THE DAYS TO
    BE,
CLAD IN A GLITTERING STRANGE-RUSTLING
    GOWN.

UPON THEIR FLAGS AND SASHES, CLOAKS
    AND COATS
NEW ASIA'S SYMBOLS, RICH EMBROIDERED
    THINGS;
(STRONG MEN, SET FREE FROM PRIDES
    THAT LEAVE US PLAIN,
BROCADED   MORE   THAN   BABYLONIAN
    KINGS:)
THEIR FACES TOUCHED WITH CULTURES
    NOW UNKNOWN,
THEIR EYES ALIGHT WITH WISDOMS WE
    DESIRE,
DOING LONG HONORS TO THE AUSTERE
    DEAD,
WITH BANNER, PANTOMIME AND SONG
    AND FIRE.
THOSE WORTHIER DAYS SHALL HAIL THEM
    FREEDOM'S SEERS:
SELF-MASTERING CHIEFS WITH GENIUS
    IN CONTROL.
AND YET, THAT MARVELLOUS WORLD SHALL
    TURN TO THIS,
TRACING SWEET FREEDOM BACK TO LIN-
    COLN'S SOUL.

WE CANNOT CONQUER TIME.

WE CANNOT CONQUER TIME. SIT DOWN,
    BREATHE SLOW,
AND MUSE A LITTLE, SINCE GREAT TIME
    IS KING.
THE MOTH AND RUST SHALL DO THEIR
    DESTINED WORK
UPON US, THOUGH WE POLISH EVERY-
    THING.
AND ALL OUR QUAINT ATTEMPTS TO BEAT
    THE CLOCK
TO TREAD TIME DOWN TO DEATH WITH
    HURRYING FEET,
SHALL SLOWLY END. WE WILL REAR HIGH
    HIS FANE,
AND COUNT HIS EVERLASTING BONDAGE
    MEET.
THE MOTH, THE RUST, THE IVY AND THE
    RAIN,
THE HAIL AND SNOW EVEN TODAY WEAR
    DOWN
EACH TOWER THAT SPEAKS OF NEWNESS
    ALL TOO WELL,
EACH POMPOUS PALACE WITH ITS GLITTER-
    ING CROWN.
THE MOTH, THE RUST, THE IVY AND THE
    RAIN,
THE HAIL AND SNOW AND WIND, WILL, AT
    THE LAST,
ENTER THE INNER HEART OF THIS OUR
    RACE,
UNTIL WE LOVE NO FUTURE LIKE THE
    PAST.

FINAL POEMS OF THE ROAD

LAZARUS AND DIVES.

WRITTEN FOR THAT RARE CREATURE, A
    PREOCCUPIED HOST.
I AM LAZARUS, POOR THEY SAY,
WAYSIDE DOGS ARE MINE FOR FRIENDS,
ON OUR SORES THE RAINS DESCENDS,
SCORN IS OURS THROUGHOUT THE DAY.

I AM LAZARUS AT YOUR GATE,
BREAD IS MINE, THE BITS THAT FALL
FROM YOUR AMPLE TABLE, ALL
CHANCE HAS SCATTERED FROM YOUR
    PLATE.
WELL CONTENT, I TAKE MY SHARE,
'TIS A SORT OF TACIT RIGHT.
NO MAN FOR MY CRUMB WILL FIGHT,
NO MAN DRIVES ME FROM THE STAIR.
DIVES, OF THE NOBLE HEART,
BY MISGIVING WORN AWAY:
WHETHER PLEASURES GO OR STAY
HOW YOU FUME AND BROOD AND START!
LAZARUS YOU NEVER SEE,
ALL THE LOAF OF LIFE YOU OWN,
MADE SO GOOD FOR YOU ALONE,
YET THIS CRUMB COMES DOWN TO ME.

A PRAYER TO ALL THE DEAD AMONG
MINE OWN PEOPLE.

ARE THESE YOUR PRESENCES, MY CLAN
    FROM HEAVEN?
ARE THESE YOUR HANDS UPON MY
    WOUNDED SOUL?
MINE OWN, MINE OWN, BLOOD OF MY
    BLOOD BE WITH ME,
FLY BY MY PATH TILL YOU HAVE MADE
    ME WHOLE!

ON THE ROAD TO NOWHERE.

ON THE ROAD TO NOWHERE
WHAT WILD OATS DID YOU SOW
WHEY YOU LEFT YOUR FATHER'S HOUSE
WITH YOUR CHEEKS AGLOW?
EYES SO STRAINED AND EAGER
TO SEE WHAT YOU MIGHT SEE?
WERE YOU THIEF OR WERE YOU FOOL
OR MOST NOBLY FREE?

WERE THE TRAMP-DAYS KNIGHTLY,
TRUE SOWING OF WILD SEED?
DID YOU DARE TO MAKE THE SONGS
VANQUISHED WORKMEN NEED?
DID YOU WASTE MUCH MONEY
TO DECK A LEPER'S FEAST?
LOVE THE TRUTH, DEFY THE CROWD,
SCANDALIZE THE PRIEST?
ON THE ROAD TO NOWHERE
WHAT WILD OATS DID YOU SOW?
STUPIDS FIND THE NOWHERE-ROAD
DUSTY GRIM AND SLOW.
ERE THEIR SOWING'S ENDED
THEY TURN THEM ON THEIR TRACK,
LOOK AT THE CATIFF CRAVEN WIGHTS
REPENTANT, HURRYING BACK!
GROWN ASHAMED OF NOWHERE
OF RAGS ENDURED FOR YEARS,
LUST FOR VELVET IN THEIR HEARTS,
PIERCED WITH MAMMON'S SPEARS.
ALL BUT A FEW FANATICS
GIVE UP THEIR DARLING GOAL,
SEEK TO BE AS OTHERS ARE,
STULTIFY THE SOUL.
REAPINGS NOW CONFRONT THEM,
GLUT THEM, OR DESTROY,
CURIOUS SEEDS, GRAIN OR WEEDS
SOWN WITH AWFUL JOY.
HURRIED IS THEIR HARVEST,
THEY MAKE SOFT PEACE WITH MEN.
PILGRIMS PASS. THEY CARE NOT,
WILL NOT TRAMP AGAIN.

OH NOWHERE, GOLDEN NOWHERE!
SAGES AND FOOLS GO ON
TO YOUR CHAOTIC OCEAN,
TO YOUR TREMENDOUS DAWN.
FAR IN YOUR FAIR DREAM-HAVEN,
IS NOTHING OR IS ALL * * *
THEY PRESS ON, SINGING, SOWING
WILD DEEDS WITHOUT RECALL!

MR. LINDSAY OFFERS THE FOLLOWING
SERMONS, TO BE PREACHED ON SHORT
NOTICE, AND WITHOUT A COLLECTION, IN
ANY CHAPEL THAT WILL OPEN ITS DOORS
AS HE PASSES BY: (1) THE GOSPEL OF
THE HEARTH. (2) THE GOSPEL OF VOL-
UNTARY POVERTY. (3) THE HOLINESS OF
BEAUTY.

THE VILLAGE MAGAZINE

Selections

THE PERSON WHO GETS THIS PACKAGE IS ASKED TO DENOUNCE LOUDLY TO HIS NEIGHBORS ANY IDEAS IN THE PROSE OR THE VERSE HE DOES NOT LIKE. AND, ON THE OTHER HAND, HE IS URGED TO CHAMPION WITH SHAMELESS ENTHUSIASM ANY OF THESE IDEAS THAT STAND THE TEST OF CLOSE INSPECTION. IN THE END I WANT YOU TO JOIN MY GANG. I DO NOT WANT TO JOIN YOURS.

NICHOLAS VACHEL LINDSAY. RHYMER AND DESIGNER
603 SOUTH FIFTH
SPRINGFIELD ILLINOIS.

248

THE VILLAGE MAGAZINE

The Village Magazine was issued ten years ago, 700 copies. As I had long planned, I placed it on the parlor tables of the rural workers of the Anti-Saloon League of Illinois, when I made speeches in their white, cross-roads churches. Some of this experience, and the education given me by these men, is hinted at in the chapter called "The Substitute for the Saloon" in "The Art of the Moving Picture".

This, the second imprint of The Village Magazine, ten years later, includes a few plates that I used for printing tracts of one sort and another about 1908-1913, here in Springfield, Illinois. Nearly every design is dated, and tells its own story in some fashion.

Pages one hundred and three to one hundred and twenty-eight contain drawings made this summer, a new editorial, and, finally, a confidential index.

In 1910 little magazines were blossoming and fading everywhere. I had seen so many fail after six months, that I began, with malice aforethought, plotting to issue but one number, put everything I desired to present at the time into it, and give it away. And so I did. I gave it away, not only throughout Central Illinois, but to citizens of Springfield, whom it greatly exasperated.

I now submit, with more emphasis, the idea of a one number magazine—that number to be steadily improved after due meditation. The ideal magazine would be as permanent as a book requiring no number two, but having a magazine's privilege of combining verse picture editorial and design into one unit, and a book's privilege of being reissued in revised editions.

A magazine is not necessarily a "periodical". The Standard Dictionary defines a magazine as: "A house, a room or a receptacle in which anything is stored, specifically a strong building for storing gunpowder and other military stores," etc., etc.

Let us go back to the original meaning of the word magazine.

CONTENTS OF AN INK BOTTLE.

N.V.L. 1910.

THE EMPTY BOATS.

WHY DO I SEE THESE EMPTY BOATS, SAILING ON AIRY SEAS?
ONE HAUNTED ME THE WHOLE NIGHT LONG, SWAYING WITH EVERY BREEZE,
RETURNING ALWAYS NEAR THE EAVES, OR BY THE SKYLIGHT GLASS;
THERE IT WILL WAIT ME MANY WEEKS, AND THEN, AT LAST, WILL PASS.

EACH SOUL IS HAUNTED BY A SHIP IN WHICH THAT SOUL MIGHT RIDE
AND CLIMB THE GLORIOUS MYSTERIES OF HEAVEN'S SILENT TIDE
IN VOYAGES THAT CHANGE THE VERY METES AND BOUNDS OF FATE —
OH EMPTY BOATS, WE ALL REFUSE, THAT BY OUR WINDOWS WAIT! NICHOLAS VACHEL LINDSAY
APRIL, 1910.

THE SHIELD OF LUCIFER

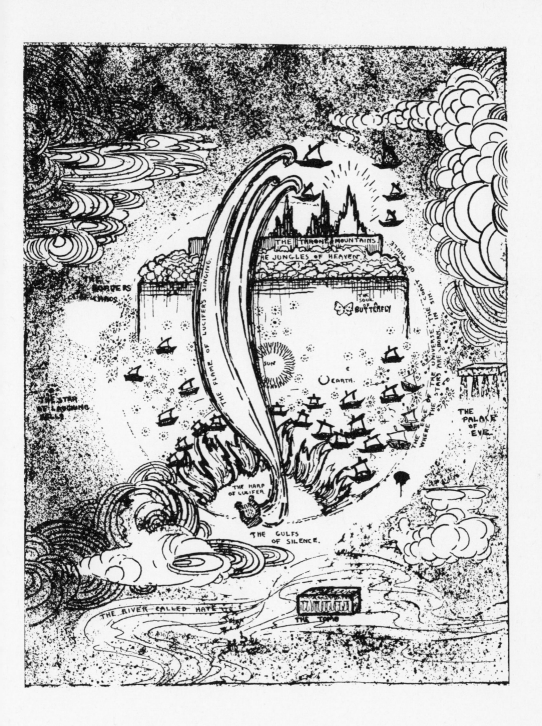

A MAP OF THE UNIVERSE ISSUED IN 1909.
THIS MAP IS ONE BEGINNING OF THE
GOLDEN BOOK OF SPRINGFIELD.

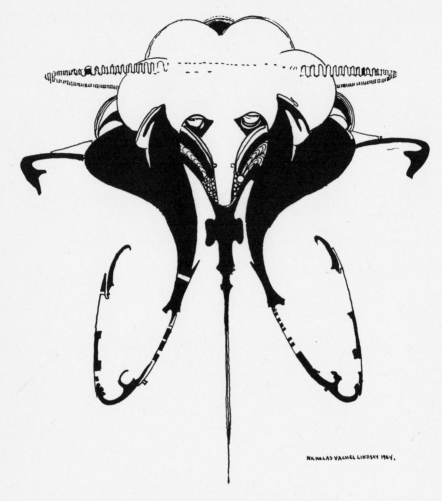

Nicholas Vachel Lindsay 1904.

THE SOUL OF A SPIDER

The thing that eats the rotting stars
   On the black sea-beach of shame
Is a giant spider's deathless soul,
   And Mammon is its name.

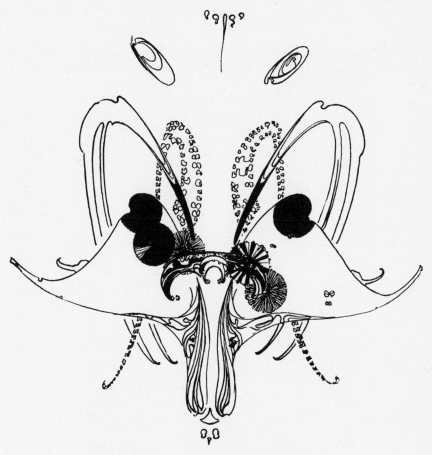

THE SOUL OF A BUTTERFLY

The thing that breaks Hell's prison bars,
    And heals the sea of shame,
Is a fragile butterfly's great soul
    And Beauty is its name.

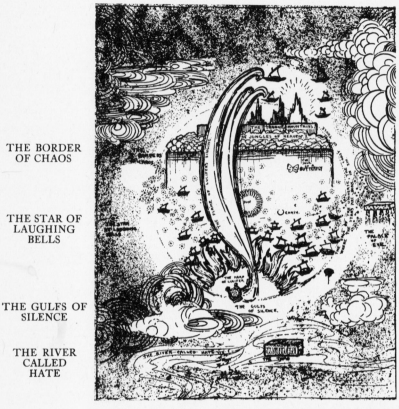

THE BORDER
OF CHAOS

THE STAR OF
LAUGHING
BELLS

THE GULFS OF
SILENCE

THE RIVER
CALLED
HATE

THE BOATS OF
THE PROPHETS
SAILING NEAR
THE THRONES
OF THE TRIN-
ITY

THE PALACE
OF EVE

THE SOUL OF A
SPIDER

THE TOMB OF
LUCIFER

A MAP OF THE UNIVERSE ISSUED IN 1909.
THIS MAP IS ONE BEGINNING OF THE
GOLDEN BOOK OF SPRINGFIELD.

THIS MAP IS USED AS THE FRONTISPIECE TO THE ILLUSTRATED COL-
LECTED POEMS, ISSUED BY MACMILLANS, 1925.

EXPLANATION OF THE MAP OF THE UNIVERSE

In the summer of 1904 I began to have some noteworthy experiences. It is plausible, I think, that for one who had so long co-ordinated drawings and poems for drawings, his religious experiences should paint themselves before him in the air. Had I been an Arabian I might have drawn the sword on the authority of the visions that came in cataracts. Even yet I cannot disabuse my mind of the faith that they were sent. I believe they were inspired, but by no means infallible. They were metaphors of the day, consolations of the hour. I determined to make them the servants, not the masters of my religious life. Though I understood mysteries and knowledge, and had not charity, I was nothing.

Being taught by that admirable, practical but unimaginative master William. M. Chase never to draw a thing till I saw it on the blank paper before me, it was only the terrible power and blaze of the pictures that came that made them unusual. In a certain corner of this room, one night, I saw the Prophets go by in gorgeous apparel. Then I wrote "A Prayer in the Jungles of Heaven." At another time, in the day by the elm in the front yard, they went by in the same robes. Yet when I wrote a story about them, I clothed them in rough penitential raiment. All through the summer I took similar liberties in the face of Hell and Heaven, determined not to be conquered by pictures in the air; I built a universe, half my own, half revealed, and put it all in a book I have destroyed, entitled "Where is Aladdin's lamp?"

The Map of the Universe, here given, is the stage of that lost drama. It deepens the metaphors of several poems. Let it be like the stage plan of *Every-man,* dear reader. Do not despise this, my little Mystery Play, all that is left of six wonderful months of eating of the flower of the Holy Ghost.

The Throne Mountains were once the dwelling place of the Trinity; but they are desolate. Only the vine of the Amaranth, the flower of the Holy Ghost, grows about his mountain throne, bearing luminous inflaming honey-flowers. Around this mountain gather the boats of the prophets. The ancient men eat this flower only. It makes them hope against hope. They prophesy a New Universe. On the plateau below are the Jungles of Heaven, empty of souls, a region of fallen palaces, rotted harps, broken crowns, swords of rusted gold. The Angels are the Missionaries of the Universe. They have gone forth to the stars to be crucified, and to be forsaken of God. Their shed blood, by transubstantiation enters the Wine jars carried by the boats of the prophets. This wine is poured as a purple mist in the paths of men. It becomes the light that never shone on sea or land, the gleam, the still small voice, the cloud of glory.

Some day Hell shall be redeemed by a storm of this wine poured down. This is just; because it was by a leaping flame from the Harp of that great Singer Lucifer, that the angels fell in love with suffering, and went forth to the stars to be forsaken of God. Thus was Lucifer King of the Universe the moment before he was cursed with eternal silence and sealed in his tomb.

Beneath the walls of Heaven is the soul of the Butterfly, which is the soul of the Earth redeemed, and on the edge of Hell is the soul of the Giant Spider, who is Mammon. East of the Universe is the Palace of Eve, whence come the perfect Brides; west of the Universe is the Star of Laughing Bells, only to be reached by the Wings of the Morning. One bell will quench all memory, all hope, all borrowed sorrow. You will have no thirst for yesterday or for the future. Wizards and witches and fairies say that by finding Aladdin's Lamp, which sleeps somewhere in the myriad treasure-pits of the Jungles of Heaven, the new Universe can be built, and all the cities of the Wise. The Genii of the lamp can be commanded to carry the Laughing Bells to every soul in the Universe, and thus redeem them all. The angels and prophets say that the New Universe comes by the power of the Wine of God, the blood of the crucified Angels. But however it come, I have a faith in the most treasured metaphor of my life that the day after the Millenium, Immanuel will sing.

THE WEDDING OF THE ROSE AND THE LOTUS.

A POEM WRITTEN ON THE NEAR-COMPLETION OF THE PANAMA CANAL, SHOWING HOW THE GENIUS OF THE WEST HERE TYPIFIED BY THE ROSE, AND THE GENIUS OF THE EAST, HERE TYPIFIED BY THE LOTUS, ARE TO BE MERGED AND MINGLED IN ONE.

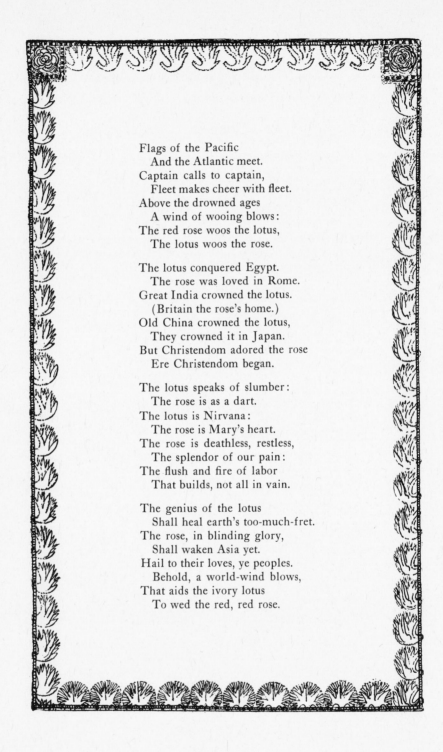

Flags of the Pacific
    And the Atlantic meet.
Captain calls to captain,
    Fleet makes cheer with fleet.
Above the drowned ages
    A wind of wooing blows:
The red rose woos the lotus,
    The lotus woos the rose.

The lotus conquered Egypt.
    The rose was loved in Rome.
Great India crowned the lotus.
    (Britain the rose's home.)
Old China crowned the lotus,
    They crowned it in Japan.
But Christendom adored the rose
    Ere Christendom began.

The lotus speaks of slumber:
    The rose is as a dart.
The lotus is Nirvana:
    The rose is Mary's heart.
The rose is deathless, restless,
    The splendor of our pain:
The flush and fire of labor
    That builds, not all in vain.

The genius of the lotus
    Shall heal earth's too-much-fret.
The rose, in blinding glory,
    Shall waken Asia yet.
Hail to their loves, ye peoples.
    Behold, a world-wind blows,
That aids the ivory lotus
    To wed the red, red rose.

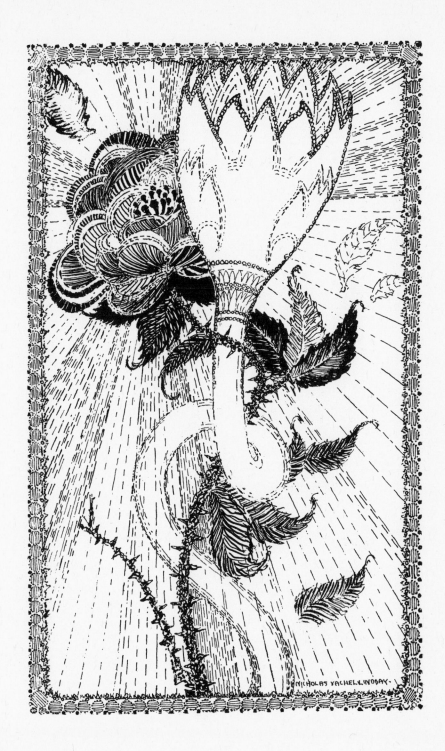

The Moon-Worms

(What the Hyena said)

The moon is but a golden skull;
She mounts the heavens now,
And moon-worms, mighty moon-worms
Are wreathed around her brow.

The moon-worms are a doughty race;
They eat her grey and golden face,
Her eye-sockets dead, and moulding head;—
These caverns are their dwelling place.

The moon-worms, serpents of the skies,
From the great hollows of her eyes
Behold our souls, and they are wise:
With tiny, keen and icy eyes
Behold how each man sins, and dies.

When earth in gold corruption lies
Long dead, the moon-worm butterflies
On cyclone wings will reach this place—
Yea, rear their brood on earth's dead face.

N.V.L. 1910.

ON THE BUILDING OF SPRINGFIELD.

LET NOT OUR TOWN BE LARGE --- REMEMBERING
THAT LITTLE ATHENS WAS THE MUSES' HOME,
THAT OXFORD RULES THE HEART OF LONDON STILL,
THAT FLORENCE GAVE THE RENAISSANCE TO ROME.

RECORD IT FOR THE GRANDSON OF YOUR SON ---
A CITY IS NOT BUILDED IN A DAY:
OUR LITTLE TOWN CANNOT COMPLETE HER SOUL
TILL COUNTLESS GENERATIONS PASS AWAY.

NOW LET EACH CHILD BE JOINED AS TO A CHURCH
TO HER PERPETUAL HOPES, EACH MAN ORDAINED;
LET EVERY STREET BE MADE A REVERENT AISLE
WHERE MUSIC GROWS, AND BEAUTY IS UNCHAINED.

LET SCIENCE AND MACHINERY AND TRADE
BE SLAVES OF HER, AND MAKE HER ALL IN ALL ---
BUILDING AGAINST OUR BLATANT, RESTLESS TIME
AN UNSEEN, SKILLFUL, MEDIAEVAL WALL.

LET EVERY CITIZEN BE RICH TOWARD GOD.
LET CHRIST, THE BEGGAR TEACH DIVINITY -
LET NO MAN RULE WHO HOLDS HIS MONEY DEAR.
LET THIS, OUR CITY, BE OUR LUXURY.

WE SHOULD BUILD PARKS THAT STUDENTS FROM AFAR
WOULD CHOOSE TO STARVE IN, RATHER THAN GO HOME ---
FAIR LITTLE SQUARES, WITH PHIDIAN ORNAMENT ---
FOOD FOR THE SPIRIT, MILK AND HONEY COMB.

SONGS SHALL BE SUNG BY US IN THAT GOOD DAY --
SONGS WE HAVE WRITTEN -- BLOOD WITHIN THE RHYME
BEATING, AS WHEN OLD ENGLAND STILL WAS GLAD,
THE PURPLE, RICH ELIZABETHAN TIME.

SAY, IS MY PROPHECY TOO FAIR AND FAR?
I ONLY KNOW, UNLESS HER FAITH BE HIGH,
THE SOUL OF THIS, OUR NINEVEH IS DOOMED,
OUR LITTLE BABYLON WILL SURELY DIE.

SOME CITY ON THE BREAST OF ILLINOIS
NO WISER AND NO BETTER AT THE START
BY FAITH SHALL RISE REDEEMED, BY FAITH SHALL RISE
BEARING THE WESTERN GLORY IN HER HEART: --

THE GENIUS OF THE MAPLE, ELM AND OAK,
THE SECRET HIDDEN IN EACH GRAIN OF CORN --
THE GLORY THAT THE PRAIRIE ANGELS SING
AT NIGHT WHEN SONS OF LIFE AND LOVE ARE BORN --

BORN BUT TO STRUGGLE, SQUALID AND ALONE,
BROKEN AND WANDERING IN THEIR EARLY YEARS.
WHEN WILL THEY MAKE OUR DUSTY STREETS THEIR GOAL,
WITHIN OUR ATTICS HIDE THEIR SACRED TEARS?

WHEN WILL THEY START OUR VULGAR BLOOD ATHRILL
WITH LIVING LANGUAGE, WORDS THAT SET US FREE?
WHEN WILL THEY MAKE A PATH OF BEAUTY CLEAR
BETWEEN OUR RICHES AND OUR LIBERTY?

WE MUST HAVE MANY LINCOLN-HEARTED MEN --
A CITY IS NOT BUILDED IN A DAY --
AND THEY MUST DO THEIR WORK, AND COME AND GO
WHILE COUNTLESS GENERATIONS PASS AWAY.

Illinois State Capitol, Springfield, with the censers of the Angels swinging over it.

THE AIRSHIP OF THE MIND.

WITHIN THE AIRSHIP, OF THE MIND WE RIDE

ABOVE OUR LAND, BOUND DOWN FROM COAST TO COAST

BY ONE STRONG NET OF RAILROAD IRON AND WIRE.

WE WATCH IF MEN OR MOTORS HURRY MOST.

ALL OF THE THINKING DONE BY TELEGRAPH!

GREAT TOWNS ONE SHOUT OF SPEED AND BRAVERY!

NO GROUP OF STATES SUFFICIENT TO ITSELF!

THEY SPEAK ONE SPEECH, ENDURE ONE SLAVERY!

OUR SHIP IS MADE, — NOT FROM THE IRON AND WIRE,

NOT 'MID THE SHRIEKING, SLAVERY AND GRIME,

NOT FROM THE MOTORS, MOST INGENIOUS THINGS

OF ALL THE QUAINT DEVICES BORN OF TIME:

THE SHIP IS MADE FROM ALL THE BLENDED SONGS

OF ALL THE HIDDEN CHOIRS OF COUNTRY MAIDS,

FROM COBWEBS GATHERED IN THE HARVEST FIELDS,

FROM FERN DEW DRIPPING IN FORGOTTEN GLADES,

FROM VIOLETS GATHERED BY THE OLD STATE ROAD,

FROM WEDDING DRESSES OF THE VILLAGE BRIDES,

FROM HOURS WHEN SPRING'S SHARP BEAUTY BREAKS THE HEART,

FROM DAYS WHEN SWEET RELIGON COMES IN TIDES: —

VAGUE TREASURES THESE, YET IN THEMSELVES WIDE WINGS

TO LIFT ALL MEN, AND TO THAT END DESIGNED.

FROM SUCH FRAIL SPIRIT-MOTORS THOUGHT WILL COME,

PEACE, AND THE SWAN-WHITE AIRSHIP OF THE MIND.

AN EDITORIAL FOR THE ART STUDENT WHO HAS
RETURNED TO THE VILLAGE.

No matter what your study, if you pursued it to the bitter end, you found yourself lured from Chicago to New York. Thence you were led on to London, Paris, Berlin or Munich. The only thing that could hold you back was lack of funds. Assuming you went this path, as so many of my acquaintances have done you finally found yourself in culture, a citizen of Europe. *❧* The first two sentences of the Gettysburg address are graven on every native soul. So you have come back all the way to the old home. Many good patriots, not knowing the treasures accumulating at the cross-roads since they left, have compromised on New York or Chicago. They are an example to you in your hours of defeat, for they are happy in the cities. Many sensitive fellows keep laughing, though they use all their strength to produce delicate, highly wrought work. To be true to democracy is also their task, as they know. They fail, but smile. *❧* It is *indeed difficult to discover the taste of the man in the street. He seems, from the standpoint of culture, to be a mechanical toy, amused by clockwork.* He is clipped to a terrible uniformity by the sharp edges of life. He knows who won the last baseball game and who may be the next president. He knows the names of the grand opera singers he has heard on the phonograph. He turns over luxuriously in his subconscious soul the tunes he has heard on the self-playing piano in front of the vaudeville theatre. He will read a poem if it is telegraphed across the country, with a good newspaper story to start it. All of his thinking is done by telegraph and fancies that are too delicate to be expressed by the comic supplement seldom reach him. Dominated by a switch-board civilization, he moves in grooves from one clock-work splendor to another. He reads the same set of magazines from New York to San Francisco. The magazines are great, yet they make for uniformity. *❧* What a task then has the conscientious art-democrat, to find the individual, delicate, immortal soul of this creature, dressed in a Hart, Schaffner and Marx suit and trying to look like a Hart, Schaffner and Marx advertisement! *For the most part, the really trained man can find little common ground.* When Poe's poems went the rounds of the newspapers, when the World's Fair stirred the land for a season, when the servant in the house had his triumph, when Markham for a moment was heard, democracy and art seemed to meet. But think of the thousands of enterprises just as fine, but lacking advertising value, or mere size, that have been scornfully ignored by Mister Hart, Schaffner-Marx! *They were poured forth with joy; by the European standard they would have been immortal. By our relentless standard, which we can never escape, they are valueless as the dollar bills of the Southern Confederacy.* *❧* The city craftsmen who have really embraced the problem of the mob, determined to be masters whether they are Orthodox or not, are to be commended. They are on the whole as well placed as the village designer, but no more so. It is a noble thing to build a successful skyscraper, but there will be the same art laughter in your heart if you give some grace to the wheat elevator at the way-station. Once in a while an O. Henry becomes a story writer, still remaining a journalist, exquisitely combining the two. But it is just as exquisite and meritorious a thing to edit the Fulton County Democrat at Lewistown. ✍ Our most conspicuous advertising and magazine artists, men of immense ingenuity turn out a sort of cover design that could be stepped on by a fire-engine horse, shot through by currents from an electric chair, run through a rolling mill, pushed off a tower or baked in a pie and come out still singing, like the four and twenty blackbirds. And in all seriousness this work has chances to survive the centuries, along with the pyramids because it expresses precisely the mood of high-class-ready-made-clothing-democracy. It is just like Chicago, where Adams meets Randolph Street. It is as near to history as anything written by Ida Tarbell. ✍ We who want to be democrats, yet avoid these phases, have an opportunity in the cross-roads that gave us birth. There we can be true to grand-father's log cabin and at the same time remember the Erectheum and the Temple of Nikko. There we meet the real citizen, three generations before he is ironed out into a mechanical toy. *His crudity is plain, but his delicacy is apparent also. His sound culture-tendencies and false tendencies can be sorted out.* At home we encounter institutions just beginning to bloom, absolutely democratic, yet silken and rich; no two villages quite alike, all with chances of developing intense uniqueness, *while all the rest of America speaks one iron speech.*✍ Of course staying at home has its drawbacks. Your work goes down, technically, through lack of the skilled criticism you once knew. You lose some chances of recognition from the growing art circles of the metropolis. *But your life is now thoroughly dedicated to the proposition that all men are created equal in taste. You are engaged in a joyous Civil War testing whether your work, or any work so conceived and so dedicated can long endure. Just as much real civilization hangs upon your success as hung upon the fighting of the private soldier at Gettysburg.* ✍ Oh, all you students that I have loved, whose work I have enviously admired, who are now back home grubbing at portraits, though they are not your specialty; or designing billboards, though they are not your divine call; or acting on the committee to paper the church and buying bad paper to please them; or back on the home newspaper that will not often print your short novels; or singing in the old choir for no salary at all; or composing advertisements in the real estate office and neglecting your lyrics; or taking charge of the Sunday School orchestra and curing them of the Moody-Sankey habit—

greeting, and God-speed to you! If you have any cherished beauty-enterprise, undertake it where you are. *You will find no better place in all America.* ✍ It is easier for me to preach than to cut the grass in my own front yard. It is easier to hand out art advice than to make a first rate irrelevant section. Maybe the interest of this work depends upon the irrelevant departments, yet there as elsewhere my lettering is rude, my drawing thin, my verse uneven. However casual the magazine, I hope you like it. Oh game and joyous crafts-man, it is likely that I will enjoy whatever *you* attempt that comes under *my* eye. Whether you are making a picture or a book, a news-paper, a tombstone or a statue, a park, a skating rink or a world's fair, I will grant you your thesis, accept your intention, laugh at your joke, frown at your sermon, find light where your ecstacy is recorded, from where the love of form is shown, line where line begins to display its power, and color where the edge of the rainbow begins to gleam.

THE CORNFIELDS.

THE CORNFIELDS RISE ABOVE MANKIND
LIFTING WHITE TORCHES TO THE BLUE
EACH SEASON NOT ASHAMED TO BE
MAGNIFICENTLY DECKED FOR YOU.

WHAT RIGHT HAVE YOU TO CALL THEM YOURS
AND IN BRUTE LUST OF RICHES BURN
WITHOUT SOME RADIANT PENANCE WROUGHT,
SOME BEAUTIFUL, DEVOUT RETURN?

271

DANCING FOR A PRIZE.

THE MILKWEED, THE SUNFLOWER AND THE ROBIN.

THE OUTLAWED MILKWEED BY THE CREEK
SCATTERING THOSE SOFT PLUMES OF DOWN
PROCLAIMS "THIS TOWN SHOULD BE OF SILK."
THE SUNFLOWER SAYS "A BLAZING CROWN
THIS TOWN SHOULD WEAR." THE ROBIN CALLS:
"LET THE TOWN HALL DELIGHT THE SUN,
STRENGTH GIVING, LOVING, FIERY, STRONG!
A ZION WHERE HIGH DEEDS ARE DONE!

ON READING OMAR KHAYYAM
DURING AN ANTI-SALOON
CAMPAIGN,
IN CENTRAL ILLINOIS.

IN THE MIDST OF THE BATTLE I TURNED,
(FOR THE THUNDERS COULD FLOURISH WITHOUT ME)
AND HID BY A ROSE-HUNG WALL,
FORGETTING THE MURDER ABOUT ME;
AND WROTE, FROM MY WOUND, ON THE STONE,
IN MIRTH, HALF PRAYER, HALF PLAY:—
"SEND ME A PICTURE BOOK,
SEND ME A SONG, TODAY."

I SAW HIM THERE BY THE WALL
WHEN I SCARCE HAD WRITTEN THE LINE
IN THE ENEMY'S COLORS DRESSED
AND THE SERPENT-STANDARD OF WINE
WRITHING ITS WITHERED LENGTH
FROM HIS GHOSTLY HANDS O'ER THE GROUND,
AND THERE BY HIS SHADOWY BREAST
THE GLORIOUS POEM I FOUND.

THIS WAS HIS WORLD-OLD CRY:
" THUS READ THE FAMOUS PRAYER:
WINE, WINE, WINE AND FLOWERS
AND CUP-BEARERS ALWAYS FAIR!"
'TWAS A BOOK OF THE SNARES OF EARTH
BORDERED IN GOLD AND BLUE,
AND I READ EACH LINE TO THE WIND
AND READ TO THE ROSES TOO:
AND THEY NODDED THEIR WOMANLY HEADS
AND TOLD TO THE WALL JUST WHY
FOR WINE OF THE EARTH MEN BLEED,
KINGDOMS AND EMPIRES DIE.

I ENVIED THE GRAPE STAINED SAGE;
(THE ROSES WERE PRAISING HIM.)
THE WAYS OF THE WORLD SEEMED GOOD
AND THE GLORY OF HEAVEN DIM.
I ENVIED THE ENDLESS KINGS
WHO FOUND GREAT PEARLS IN THE MIRE
WHO BOUGHT WITH THE NATION'S LIFE
THE CUP OF DELICIOUS FIRE.

BUT THE WINE OF GOD CAME DOWN,
AND I DRANK IT OUT OF THE AIR.
(FAIR IS THE SERPENT-CUP
BUT THE CUP OF GOD MORE FAIR.)
THE WINE OF GOD CAME DOWN
THAT MAKES NO DRINKER TO WEEP.
AND I WENT BACK TO BATTLE AGAIN
LEAVING THE SINGER ASLEEP.

CONCERNING THE ACORNS
ON THE COVER,
AND THROUGH THE BOOK.

"GREAT OAKS FROM LITTLE ACORNS GROW,"
EACH ACORN IS A MAGAZINE
OF LEAVES AND TWIGS IN EMBRYO:
THE STORMIEST FOREST EVER SEEN
WAS ONCE A HICKORY NUT OR SO,
A MAPLE SEED SOME BIRD LET GO,
A BITTER ACORN, BROWN AND GREEN.

MAYBE THIS VILLAGE MAGAZINE
WILL SOME VAST TREE OF FANCY BRING
WHEN YOU AND I ON CRUTCHES LEAN,
GROWN GRAY AND LOST TO EVERYTHING.

DOWN DROPS THE ACORN, HARD AND MEAN.
LET GOOD KINE EAT IT IF THEY WILL,
LET SWINE AND SWINEHERDS DEEM IT SWEET,
LET FAIRIES NIBBLE IT, UNSEEN,
LET SQUIRRELS FIND FATNESS IN ITS MEAT,
BUT IF ALL LIFE SHALL GIVE IT SCORN
AND ALL THINGS TREAD IT UNDERFEET,
A TITAN OAK SHALL RISE COMPLETE
SHELTERING BIRDS THAT GREET THE MORN.

ROUTINE is a beast to be slain. It is the deadliest child of our civilization. Though there is many an apparent economic r e a s on for industrial trouble, the routine which is the result of making men the servants of endlessly uniform motions, is far more responsible for discontent and riot. The nervous system goes on a strike against machinery long before the union declares a walk-out.

I myself am on a strike, that I hope will last for some time. Unless I can write a good personal longhand letter, either a blessing or a cursing, I do not answer letters. I cannot bear to write a machine letter to anyone.

When the beast of routine is wounded, if not slain, one hundred years hence, most all men and women of the same general disposition and taste for variety, who value each other, will live in some one village, say such a village as Springfield, and most meetings and conversations will be casual street-corner or park garden encounters, and letters will be for the most part abolished. Meanwhile, with a hundred dear friends, how can I write a hundred long letters every week as I desire?

I hope that this second imprint of The Village Magazine will be accepted as a longhand letter when I send it to people to whom I have been owing confidential communications for months. That it is indeed confidential is proved by the fact that I print here things impossible to put into books formally issued, or recitals formally staged.

Meanwhile, picture the man who draws these pictures, sitting before some Springfield fireplace in winter, or walking in some Springfield garden of the summer, watching the prophetic vision of the slaying of the beast of routine. One way my most intimate friends may help me, if I may be so personal, in the slaying of the beast of routine, is in the matter of reciting. I have sworn off going to women's clubs, because the young local poets seldom come, and the clubs generally refuse to act as patrons of the colleges or high schools, where the young poets are to be found. Also I prefer hostesses who do their own work, and who also read. Almost any college professor's wife is this sort, but the women's clubs hate such people with a deadly hatred. They prefer to thrust me among hostesses where there is much tea, a smothering of servants, and if there are husbands present, they are the kind of business men who find their chief nourishment in the full page advertisements of office supplies in the back of The Literary Digest, and the Saturday Evening Post. Their only idealism is to keep wives like these supplied with tea, poets, and servants, while they themselves, as good business men, keep on looking like planks of the Republican platform, every minute, and attending peppy business men's banquets.

In spite of my rough remarks about letters, *write to me,* here in Springfield, if you want me to recite for you. If I do not answer it is a sign I cannot come.

I have sworn off lecture bureaus of any sort, because they send me to people who put me on lecture courses, where I am called upon to ape myself, and parrot myself, and recite my oldest verses for an audience that has not read anyone's verses, and has not the least idea of reading mine, new or old. Also lecture bureaus and lecture courses expect a man to perform in the town eight to nine-thirty P. M., or three to four-thirty P. M., and sneak out of town without the town finding out anything about him, or his finding out anything about the town. I infinitely prefer to stay in Springfield, sing for my supper my newest pieces, for my oldest and dearest friends, or, when that palls, beg from door to door as of old.

I took to the road once, long ago, because people said if I stayed rhymer and artist I would be a beggar and die in the poor house. My most intimate friends prophesied it incessantly for years, after nourishing themselves on business men's clubs and office supply advertisements. Therefore, in no sentimental mood, but actually to try out this beggary and deliberately calling myself *"a beggar to the end of my days,"* I took to the road, and tried, as it were, the "poor-house" at its worst, that I might get used to it.

People are far too sentimental about my begging days, and talk as though they were over. I stand ready to beg tomorrow and to the end of the chapter, rather than write a line I do not want to write, recite for a routine audience, or go through any parrot or ape performances, even if am parroting and aping what I myself happened to be, twenty-four hours ago.

WAR BULLETIN
NUMBER ONE

By Nicholas Vachel Lindsay   SPRINGFIELD, ILL., JULY 19 1909   Price 5 Cents

Why a War Bulletin?

I have spent a great part of my few years fighting a soul battle for absolute liberty, for freedom from obligation, ease of conscience; independence from commercialism. I think I am farther from slavery than most men. But I have not complete freedom of speech. In my daily round of work I find myself taking counsel to please the stupid, the bigoted, the conservative, the impatient, the cheap. A good part of the time I can please these people, having a great deal in common with all of them.—but—

The things that go into the War Bulletin please me only. To the Devil with you, average reader. To Gehenna with your stupidity, your bigotry, your conservatism, your cheapness and your impatience!

In each new Bulletin the war shall go faster and further. War! War! War!

The Golden-Faced People

A Story of the Chinese Conquest of America

And yet it is not a Story. It is an Essay. All purely literary critics pray consider yourselves defied. When you have read the piece twice you may write to me and say what you think the moral is.

He was a Laundryman who ironed shirts superbly, yet as though it were a mere incident. His picked English showed him to be no ordinary Coolie. I thought we had been friends for some months. But now old Yellow-Arms clutched my week's washing because I had lost my half of his red ticket. I showed him for the tenth time the name on the linen. I was in a hurry to dress for the banquet. Pushing the money toward him, I jumped for the exit with my goods. He turned out the gas. I heard him scramble over the counter. He was between me and the door. He hit me with the handle of his broom. I thought then that I made for the alley through the side entrance.

*   *   *   *   *   *   *

I found myself in a long iron-floored passage, thick with yellow fog. Just as suddenly I was in a packed assembly room where the walls blazed with dragon embroidered lanterns. I turned around. The door of iron behind me was closed. My pursuer was not in sight.

The place looked like a sort of Heathen Temple, But no—the next thing that caught my eye was the Phrase *"In the year of Christ."* It appeared that this fantastic gathering was about to dedicate with speeches and ceremonies, a tablet inscribed, "In the year of Christ two thousand eight hundred and nine Lin Kon was born. This memorial is set up on the one hundreth anniversary of his birth, in honor of his meritorious and superior career. He was the emancipator of the white man."

The shirt washer had hit me pretty hard. He had knocked me through that iron door into the next Millennium. A person quite like him sat in the pew at one side of the platform. Despite the crowd, the rest of his bench was empty. He blinked there, in surprising majesty.

I was being escorted toward the tablet. I was being introduced to half a score of speakers of the evening, there grouped. Then I was proclaimed to the audience as one who had studied the Chinese conquest with zeal. I laid down my laundry bundle. I was in a whirlwind of astonishing impressions. And it was no longer a bundle, but had shrunk into a manuscript in my own handwriting. I opened it. I read to the crowd something after this fashion:

"When our fathers taught the Golden People mechanics, in the sordid ages of the world, the White Man was the leader of Civilization." There was a mighty cheer. The audience rose, a kaleidoscope of whirling colors. Gongs were beaten. Fans were thumped against the seats till they were splinters. I continued: "Our fathers were not scared, when the Golden Men instituted their thorough-going compulsory education, nor when they put up their immortal Universities from Canton to Lhassa. But that was the crucial hour, the pivot of history. Then in the Chinese Psychology, the religion of Science took the place of the religion of learning, which had been with them from the days of Shen and Yao. In their laboratories were hatched the medical lodges and in-

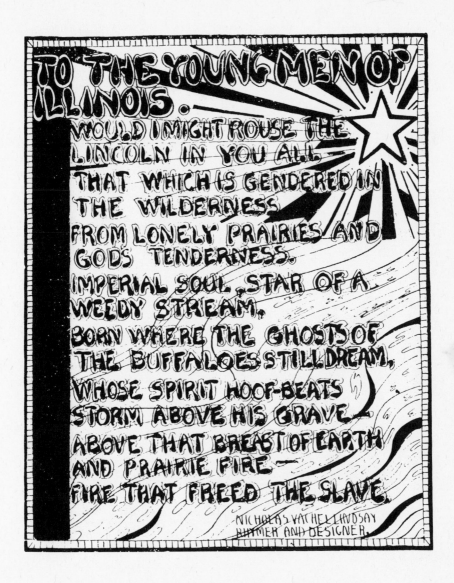

TO THE YOUNG MEN OF
ILLINOIS.
WOULD I MIGHT ROUSE THE
LINCOLN IN YOU ALL.
THAT WHICH IS GENDERED IN
THE WILDERNESS
FROM LONELY PRAIRIES AND
GODS TENDERNESS.
IMPERIAL SOUL, STAR OF A
WEEDY STREAM,
BORN WHERE THE GHOSTS OF
THE BUFFALOES STILL DREAM,
WHOSE SPIRIT HOOF-BEATS
STORM ABOVE HIS GRAVE,
ABOVE THAT BREAST OF EARTH
AND PRAIRIE FIRE—
FIRE THAT FREED THE SLAVE.

NICHOLAS VACHEL LINDSAY
RHYMER AND DESIGNER.

WHO WILL BE THE NEXT BRAVE DREAMER?

ROOSEVELT 1840-
ITO
TOLSTOI 1828-
WHITMAN 1819 TO 1892
EMERSON 1803 TO 1882

RAMESES II 1300±
MOSES 1300±
HOMER 1000±
ZOROASTER 1000±
ASSHURBANIPAL 667 TO 626
CYRUS 558 TO 529

CONFUCIUS 550 TO 478
BUDDHA 480 TO 400

PERICLES 495 TO 429
PHIDIAS 500 TO
SOCRATES 430 471
PLATO 399 427 TO 347
ARISTOTLE 384 TO 322
PRAXITELES 400 TO 336
ALEXANDER 356 TO 323
HANNIBAL 247 TO 183
CAESAR 100 TO 44 B.C.
M. AURELIUS
CONSTANTINE
ST. PAUL
JUSTINIAN
ST. AUGUSTINE
MOHAMMED
GREGORY VII
ST. DOMINIC
CHARLEMAGNE
WILLIAM THE NORMAN

RODIN 1840-
MONET 1840-
WHISTLER 1834 TO 1903
WATTS 1817 TO 1907
EDISON 1847-
PASTEUR 1822 TO 1895
DARWIN 1809 TO 1882
LINCOLN 1809 TO 1865
BISMARCK 1815 TO 1898
WASHINGTON 1732 TO 99
MIRABEAU 1749 TO 91
CROMWELL 1599 TO 1658
MILTON 1608 TO 1674-
GALILEO 1564 TO 1642

IYEYASU 1607 TO
REMBRANDT 1594 TO 1669
VELASQUEZ 1599 TO
WILLIAM OF ORANGE 1533 TO 84
SHAKESPEARE 1564 TO 1616
LOYOLA 1491 TO 1554
LUTHER 1483 TO 1546
DÜRER 1471 TO 1528
TITIAN 1477 TO 1576
MICHAELANGELO 1475 TO 1564
DANTE
SAVONAROLA 1452 TO 1498
ST. FRANCIS
COLUMBUS

282

SELECTED BIBLIOGRAPHY

POETRY

General William Booth Enters into Heaven. New York, 1913, 1916.
The Congo and Other Poems. New York, 1914.
The Chinese Nightingale and Other Poems. New York, 1917.
The Daniel Jazz and Other Poems. London, 1920.
The Golden Whales of California and Other Rhymes in the American Language. New York, 1920.
Collected Poems. New York, 1923, 1925, 1959.
Going-to-the-Sun. New York, London, 1923.
The Candle in the Cabin. New York, London, 1926.
Going-to-the-Stars. New York, London, 1926.
Johnny Appleseed and Other Poems, New York, 1928.
Every Soul Is a Circus. New York, 1929.
Selected Poems, ed. Hazelton Spencer. New York, 1931.
Selected Poems, ed. Mark Harris. New York, 1963.

PROSE

Adventures While Preaching the Gospel of Beauty. New York, 1914, 1921.
The Art of the Moving Picture. New York, 1915, 1922.
A Handy Guide for Beggars, Especially Those of the Poetic Fraternity. . . . New York, 1916.
The Golden Book of Springfield. New York, 1920.
Letters of Nicholas Vachel Lindsay to A. Joseph Armstrong, ed. A. Joseph Armstrong. Waco, 1940.

PAMPHLETS AND BROADSIDES

Throughout his life, and especially before 1912, Lindsay designed and published at his own expense many fugitive pieces in the form of leaflets, broadsides, tracts, pamphlets, cards and announcements.

He chose to include his favorite examples from among these in his three editions of *The Village Magazine*, the first published in 1910 (76 pp.) the second in 1920 (128 pp.) and the third in 1925 (169 pp.)

The first complete bibliography is now being prepared, by Mr. Cecil K. Byrd, of the Indiana University Library, Bloomington, Illinois.

Among the important collections of Lindsay's work are the Melcher-

Lindsay Collection at the Indiana University Library and The George Matthew Adams Vachel Lindsay Collection at Dartmouth College Library, Hanover, New Hampshire. The most important is the C. Waller Barrett Collection at the University of Virginia, Charlottesville, Virginia, which comprises the entire Lindsay Archives, acquired from Mrs. Lindsay.

WRITINGS ON LINDSAY

Graham, Stephen. *Tramping with a Poet in the Rockies.* New York, 1922.

Harris, Mark. *City of Discontent.* Indianapolis, 1952.

Kreymberg, Alfred. "Exit Vachel Lindsay—Enter Ernest Hemingway," *Literary Review*, II (Winter 1957–58), 208–219.

Masters, Edgar Lee. *Vachel Lindsay: A Poet in America.* New York, 1935.

Orel, Harold. "Vachel Lindsay and the Blood of the Lamb." *University of Kansas City Review*, XXV (Autumn 1958), 13–17.

Putzel, Max. *The Man in the Mirror: William Marion Reedy and His Magazine.* Cambridge, 1963. Chapter XVI, 177–192.

Ruggles, Eleanor. *The West-going Heart: A Life of Vachel Lindsay.* New York, 1959.

Viereck, Peter. "The Crack-Up of American Optimism: Vachel Lindsay, The Dante of the Fundamentalists," *Modern Age.* IV (Summer 1960), 269–284.

Warren, Austin. "The Case of Vachel Lindsay," *Accent*, VI (Summer 1946), 230–239.

Whipple, T. K. *Spokesmen.* New York, 1928; Berkeley, 1963. Chapter IX, 184–207.

Yatron, Michael. *America's Literary Revolt.* New York: Philosophical Library, 1959.

ACKNOWLEDGEMENTS

We wish to express our thanks and appreciation to the Houghton Library of Harvard University, the New York Public Library, and the Beinecke Library of Yale University for their cooperation in allowing reproductions in this book to be made from copies of publications in their collections.

DESIGNED BY EDITH McKEON

COMPOSITION BY THE STINEHOUR PRESS

PRINTED BY THE NIMROD PRESS

BOUND BY RUSSELL RUTTER

X66125

Lindsay, Nicholas Vachel, 1879–1931.
  Adventures, rhymes & designs. With an essay by Robert
F. Sayre. New York, Eakins Press ₍1968₎

  287 p. illus., facsims., port. 24 cm. $7.95

  Bibliographical references included in "Notes" (p. 41)

  CONTENTS.—Adventures while preaching the gospel of beauty.—
The village improvement parade.—Rhymes to be traded for bread.—
The village magazine.—Bibliography (p. 283–284).

  I. Sayre, Robert F. II. Title.

  PS3523.I58A6   1968   818'.5'209   68–27399

Library of Congress   ₍3₎

THE GOSPE[

BEING THE NEW "CREED OF A BEGGAR" BY THA[
SAY. PRINTED FOR HIS PERSONAL FRIENDS IN HIS [
TION TO CARRY THIS GOSPEL ACROSS THE COUNTRY[

I. (PROLOGUE.) I COME TO YOU PENNILESS AN[
RELIGIOUS IDEA. THE IDEA DOES NOT SAY "NO" TO[
LET THE DENOMINATION TO WHICH YOU NOW BELO[
OR "THE CHURCH OF THE OPEN SKY." * * * THE C[
AND THE LOVE OF GOD.

II. THE NEW LOCALISM.) THE THINGS MOST WO[
WE SHOULD MAKE OUR OWN HOME AND NEIGHBOR[
THE HOLIEST IN THE WORLD. THE CHILDREN NOW[
ARCHITECTS OR PARK ARCHITECTS OR TEACHERS OF [
ISTS OR POETS OR STORY-WRITERS OR CRAFTSMEN OR[
THEY SHOULD FIND THEIR TALENT AND NURSE IT [
BLE APPLICATION TO ART-THEORY OF THE THOUGHTS[
GETYSBURG ADDRESS. THEY SHOULD, IF LED BY TH[
OF THE SECRET OF DEMOCRATIC BEAUTY WITH THEIR[
WITH THE RIGHTEOUSNESS OF GOD. THEN THEY SHOU[
HOOD AND GATHER A LITTLE CIRCLE OF THEIR OWN[
THE NEIGHBORHOOD AND HOME MORE BEAUTIFUL A[
 * * * THEY SHOULD LABOR IN THEIR LITTLE C[
IN THEIR DARKEST HOURS THEY SHOULD BE MADE S[
NEIGHBORHOOD AND THE PASSION FOR A COMPLETEL[
BE THAT JOY IN BEAUTY WHICH NO WOUNDS CAN TA[
NO CRUCIFIXION CAN END.

Lindsay's original leaflet